Learning TypeScript 5

Go beyond Javascript to build more maintainable and robust web applications for large-scale projects

Anna Richter

Copyright © 2024 by GitforGits

All rights reserved. This book is protected under copyright laws and no part of it may be reproduced or transmitted in any form or by any means, electronic or mechanical, including photocopying, recording, or by any information storage and retrieval system, without the prior written permission of the publisher. Any unauthorized reproduction, distribution, or transmission of this work may result in civil and criminal penalties and will be dealt with in the respective jurisdiction at anywhere in India, in accordance with the applicable copyright laws.

Published by: GitforGits

Publisher: Sonal Dhandre

www.gitforgits.com

support@gitforgits.com

Printed in India

First Printing: April 2024

ISBN: 978-8119177530

Cover Design by: Kitten Publishing

For permission to use material from this book, please contact GitforGits at support@gitforgits.com.

Prologue

Developers like me, who have spent years honing our JavaScript skills, know the joy of making apps that users adore. I've also experienced the frustration of tracking down obscure bugs caused by dynamic typing. That's why I decided to dive into TypeScript and see how it can improve both our development process and our finished products.

One day, while working on a complex JavaScript project, I found myself buried in a pile of code, trying to figure out a bug that was driving my team crazy. It was the type of bug that would disappear when you looked at it, only to reappearance when you thought it had vanished. After hours of debugging, I discovered it was due to a simple type mismatch. A small error with serious consequences. That was my a-ha moment. I realized I needed a tool to help me identify these issues early in the development process. I was excited and curious when I first started learning TypeScript. Initially, the concept of static typing seemed intimidating, but I quickly realized its value in producing more reliable and maintainable code. TypeScript serves as a helpful assistant, guiding you to write code that is more structured and predictable. It enables you to identify errors during development rather than waiting for them to appear unexpectedly in production. This means spending less time fixing bugs and more time creating features that users will enjoy.

I began using TypeScript on a side project, a small web app for tracking personal goals. It started as a simple tool to remind me to stay on top of my tasks, but as I worked on it, I realized TypeScript was helping me write cleaner, more organized code. The app became more complex, and TypeScript helped me manage that complexity by allowing me to define clear interfaces and data structures. The code became more readable and understandable, not only to me but also to those who looked at it. Working on this project taught me how to use TypeScript to organize a disorganized codebase into a polished work of art. I felt confident adding new features without worrying about breaking existing functionality. My app was more than just a personal success; it demonstrated TypeScript's power. As I shared the app with friends and colleagues, I realized how it could help others improve their projects, too. This motivated me to share what I'd learned and write this book.

In this "Learning TypeScript 5" book, I want to make the transition from JavaScript to TypeScript as smooth as possible. This book is more than a technical guide; it's a conversation between you and me about how TypeScript can improve your coding skills and project outcomes. We'll start with the fundamentals: configuring your environment and understanding the syntax. Then we'll go over more advanced topics like type narrowing and asynchronous programming. Each chapter builds upon the previous one, ensuring that you have a thorough understanding of TypeScript's capabilities. I wrote this book to make TypeScript more accessible and enjoyable. Whether you're an experienced JavaScript developer or new to coding, you'll find useful examples and real-world applications that demonstrate TypeScript's benefits. This book will provide you with the tools and knowledge you need to write more efficient, error-free code.

Content

Preface .... *ix*
GitforGits .... *xi*
Acknowledgement .... *xii*

Chapter 1: Introduction to TypeScript 1

Chapter Overview *2*

Understanding TypeScript and Its Benefits *2*
   History and Evolution of TypeScript 2
   Key Features and Capabilities of TypeScript 3
   Why TypeScript over JavaScript? 3
   Classic Use-case: Airbnb's Migration to TypeScript 4

Setting up TypeScript Environment *4*
   Installing TypeScript and Node.js on Windows 4
   Configuring TypeScript Compiler 5
   Installing and Setting up Visual Studio Code 7

Basic TypeScript Syntax *8*
   Variables and Constants 8
   Data Types 9
   Type Annotations 11
   Comparing TypeScript to JavaScript Syntax 11

Type Annotations and Inference *14*
   Explicit Type Annotations 14
   Type Inference by Compiler 16

Compiling TypeScript to JavaScript *19*
   What is Compilation? 19
   The Compilation Process 20
   'tsc' Command 20
   Configuring tsconfig.json 21

Summary *23*

Chapter 2: Working with Basic Types 25

Chapter Overview *26*

Number, String, and Boolean Types 26
Declaring Number Variables 26
Using Strings 28
Constructing Boolean Logics and Conditions 29

Arrays and Tuples 30
Declaring and Initializing Arrays 30
Using Tuples 31
Array Methods and Operations 33

Enum Types 36
Defining Enums 36
Enum Members and Values 37

Any, Unknown, and Void Types 40
'any' Type 40
'unknown' Type 41
'void' Type 41
Sample Program 42

Null and Undefined 44
Managing Null and Undefined Values 44
Exploring Type Guards 45
Understanding Optional Chaining and Nullish Coalescing 46

Summary 48

Chapter 3: Functions in TypeScript 50

Chapter Overview 51

Function Types and Signatures 51
Regular Functions 51
Function Expressions 52
Arrow Functions 53
Function Signatures and Call Signatures 54

Optional and Default Parameters 56
Optional Parameters 56
Default Parameter Values 57
Multiple Default Parameters 58
Rest Parameters and Variadic Functions 60
Creating Variadic Functions 61
Combining Rest Parameters with Other Parameters 62

Function Overloads 62
What is an Overloaded Function? 63
Sample Program 63
Function Overloads with Multiple Parameters 65

Arrow, Callback and Higher-Order Functions *67*
    Arrow Functions 67
    Callback Functions 70
    Higher-Order Functions 73

Summary *75*

Chapter 4: Complex Types and Union Types 77

Chapter Overview *78*

Union and Intersection Types *78*
    Union Types 78
    Intersection Types 81
    Sample Program 83

Type Guards and Type Assertions *85*
    Type Guards 85
    Type Assertions 89

Literal Types and Type Aliases *92*
    Literal Types 92
    Type Aliases 94
    Sample Program 98

Nullable Types and Optional Properties *100*
    Nullable Types 100
    Optional Properties 103
    Optional Chaining 107
    Sample Program 109

Advanced Object Types *112*
    Index Signatures 112
    Recursive Types 115
    Sample Program 118

Summary *122*

Chapter 5: Classes and Interfaces 123

Chapter Overview *124*

Working with Classes *124*
    Creating Classes 124
    Defining Class Constructors and Methods 126
    Public, Private, and Protected Modifiers 130
    Sample Program 135

Class Inheritance and Modifiers *137*
    Implementing Inheritance 137

Defining Abstract Classes 140
Applying Access Modifiers in Inheritance 144
Sample Program 147

Interfaces in Action *152*
Defining an Interface 152
Implementing Interfaces in Classes 153
Optional Properties 157
Readonly Properties 160
Sample Program 162

Extending Interfaces *168*
Extending Interfaces 168
Combining Interfaces with Intersection Types 172
Sample Program 175

Summary *184*

Chapter 6: Modules and Namespaces 185

Chapter Overview *186*

Introduction to Modules *186*
Module Structure 186
Module Working in ES6 187
Working of Modules 190

Importing and Exporting Modules *193*
Exporting Modules 193
Importing Modules 196
Aliasing Imports 197

Combining Default and Named Exports *199*

Working with Namespaces *203*
Defining Namespaces 203
Nested Namespaces 205
Sample Program 207

Summary *211*

Chapter 7: TypeScript in Practice 213

Chapter Overview *214*

Integrating TypeScript with Angular *214*
Setting up Angular Project 214
Utilizing TypeScript in Angular Components 215
Utilizing TypeScript in Angular Services 217
Integrating TypeScript with Angular Features 221

Integrating TypeScript with React 223
Setting up React with TypeScript 223
Utilizing TypeScript in React Components 224
Utilizing TypeScript with React Hooks 228
Utilizing TypeScript with React Context 231

Migrating JavaScript Applications to TypeScript 235
Migration Process 236
Troubleshooting Common Migration Issues 240
Implementing Migration 241

Testing TypeScript Applications 244
Overview 244
Introduction to Jest 244
Writing Unit Test Scripts 246
Writing Integration Test Scripts 247

Summary 250

Chapter 8: Runtime Behavior and Type Checking 252

Chapter Overview 253

Understanding Runtime Type Checking 253
What is Type Checking? 253
Performing Type Checking at Runtime 254
Troubleshooting and Managing Type Errors 256

Type Narrowing Techniques 261
What is Type Narrowing? 261
Type Narrowing Techniques 262

Handling Asynchronous Code 269
Introduction to Promises 269
Async/Await Syntax 271
Troubleshooting Errors in Asynchronous Code 273

Exception Management 277
Introduction to Try/Catch Blocks 277
Creating Custom Error Classes 279

Summary 283

Index 285

Epilogue 287

Preface

Programmers familiar with JavaScript who wish to learn more about TypeScript version 5.0 will find this book to be a resource of great value This book is ideal for developers who want to improve their front-end programming skills and integrate TypeScript with popular frameworks such as Angular and React. With clear explanations and hands-on examples, this book makes the transition from JavaScript to TypeScript easy and enjoyable.

The book covers fundamental concepts such as static typing, type checking, and type inference, which will help you write more reliable and maintainable code. You'll learn how to use TypeScript's features to improve your development process, reduce bugs, and increase code quality. You'll learn about TypeScript's advanced features, such as interfaces, modules, and type narrowing techniques, through hands-on examples. To help you write more efficient and clean code, this book also covers how to use async/await and Promises to deal with asynchronous operations.

"Learning TypeScript 5" offers solutions and troubleshooting techniques for the most common TypeScript challenges that developers face. You'll find out how to make your own error classes for different situations and how to use TypeScript's try/catch blocks to manage errors effectively. Integrating TypeScript with preexisting JavaScript applications, configuring the TypeScript compiler, and setting up TypeScript projects are all covered in the book. After finishing this book, you will have the knowledge and abilities to create scalable applications with TypeScript and work with frameworks such as Angular and React with ease. Whether you're starting a new project or upgrading an existing one, "Learning TypeScript 5" provides useful insights and practical knowledge to help you improve your development skills and take your programming to the next level.

In this book you will learn how to:

- Learn TypeScript's static typing to make your JavaScript code more reliable and less prone to mistakes.

- Make the switch from JavaScript to TypeScript with ease thanks to the detailed instructions and numerous examples.

- Use TypeScript with Angular and React to create scalable, reliable web apps.

- Create flawless code with TypeScript's type narrowing and control flow analysis.

- Maximize productivity in development and application speed by integrating TypeScript with Angular and React.

- Write cleaner, and more readable scripts with Promises and async/await.

- Use try/catch and other error handling methods to implement a robust system for managing errors.
- Master TypeScript's union types, interfaces, and modules for code organization.
- Maximize code quality with TypeScript's robust testing strategies and robust type-checking capabilities.

GitforGits

Prerequisites

This book is ideal for developers who want to improve their front-end programming skills and integrate TypeScript with popular frameworks such as Angular and React. With clear explanations and hands-on examples, this book makes the transition from JavaScript to TypeScript easy and enjoyable.

Codes Usage

Are you in need of some helpful code examples to assist you in your programming and documentation? Look no further! Our book offers a wealth of supplemental material, including code examples and exercises.

Not only is this book here to aid you in getting your job done, but you have our permission to use the example code in your programs and documentation. However, please note that if you are reproducing a significant portion of the code, we do require you to contact us for permission.

But don't worry, using several chunks of code from this book in your program or answering a question by citing our book and quoting example code does not require permission. But if you do choose to give credit, an attribution typically includes the title, author, publisher, and ISBN. For example, "Learning TypeScript 5 by Anna Richter".

If you are unsure whether your intended use of the code examples falls under fair use or the permissions outlined above, please do not hesitate to reach out to us at support@gitforgits.com.

We are happy to assist and clarify any concerns.

Acknowledgement

I owe a tremendous debt of gratitude to GitforGits, for their unflagging enthusiasm and wise counsel throughout the entire process of writing this book. Their knowledge and careful editing helped make sure the piece was useful for people of all reading levels and comprehension skills. In addition, I'd like to thank everyone involved in the publishing process for their efforts in making this book a reality. Their efforts, from copyediting to advertising, made the project what it is today.

Finally, I'd like to express my gratitude to everyone who has shown me unconditional love and encouragement throughout my life. Their support was crucial to the completion of this book. I appreciate your help with this endeavour and your continued interest in my career.

Chapter 1: Introduction to TypeScript

Chapter Overview

The robust superset of JavaScript, TypeScript, is the subject of our first learning in this chapter. We will start by learning what TypeScript is and why it's become such an important tool for modern web development. This section will highlight the key benefits of using TypeScript, such as improved code quality, a better developer experience, and the ability to detect errors early in the development process.

Next, we will walk you through the process of setting up your TypeScript development environment on a Windows system. This entails installing the necessary tools, such as Node.js and Visual Studio Code, configuring the TypeScript compiler, and ensuring that everything is properly set up to begin writing TypeScript code. By the end of this section, you should have a fully functional TypeScript environment ready to code. We will then go over the fundamental syntax of TypeScript. This section covers the fundamental aspects of TypeScript, such as variables, data types, and basic constructs that distinguish it from JavaScript. You'll learn how to write simple TypeScript programs as well as the syntax enhancements available in TypeScript, which will make your code more robust and maintainable.

Finally, we look at type annotations and inference, which are two core TypeScript features that add static typing to your code. You will learn how to explicitly define types and how TypeScript can automatically infer types, allowing you to write cleaner and more predictable code. We also go over how to compile TypeScript into JavaScript, ensuring compatibility across all JavaScript environments. This chapter lays the groundwork for the more advanced topics and practical applications that will follow as you progress through the book.

Understanding TypeScript and Its Benefits

History and Evolution of TypeScript

TypeScript was introduced by Microsoft in 2012, spearheaded by Anders Hejlsberg, the lead architect behind C# and creator of Delphi and Turbo Pascal. Recognizing the limitations and complexities faced by developers with JavaScript, especially in large-scale applications, Microsoft aimed to create a superset of JavaScript that provided optional static typing, interfaces, and advanced tooling. The goal was to enhance productivity and maintainability, particularly in enterprise environments where robust, scalable applications were a necessity.

From its initial release, TypeScript quickly gained traction within the developer community. Early versions focused on providing a strong type system and tooling support, but as the language matured, it incorporated more sophisticated features such as decorators, async/await, and improved type inference. The integration with popular frameworks like Angular further accelerated its adoption, making TypeScript an integral part of modern web development. The evolution of TypeScript has been marked by regular updates, each introducing new features and improvements that keep it aligned with the latest advancements in JavaScript and the needs of the developer community.

Key Features and Capabilities of TypeScript

TypeScript's primary strength lies in its ability to provide optional static typing. This feature allows developers to define types for variables, function parameters, and return values, enabling early detection of type-related errors. Unlike JavaScript, where type-related issues are often discovered at runtime, TypeScript's type system helps catch these issues during the development phase, significantly reducing the likelihood of bugs in production.

TypeScript supports modern JavaScript features and ensures compatibility with the latest ECMAScript standards. This includes support for ES6/ES7 features such as classes, modules, and arrow functions, among others. By compiling TypeScript code to JavaScript, developers can leverage these features even in environments that do not natively support the latest JavaScript standards.

Another notable feature is TypeScript's tooling support. Integrated development environments (IDEs) like Visual Studio Code offer rich TypeScript support, including intelligent code completion, navigation, and refactoring. This enhances the development experience, making it easier to write, read, and maintain TypeScript code.

TypeScript also offers advanced features such as generics, which enable the creation of reusable and type-safe components, and decorators, which provide a way to add metadata to classes and methods. These features make TypeScript a powerful tool for building large and complex applications, ensuring that the code remains clean, maintainable, and scalable.

Why TypeScript over JavaScript?

TypeScript offers several advantages over JavaScript, primarily through its type system. The static typing helps prevent common errors that occur due to type mismatches. For instance, operations on incompatible types, which would cause runtime errors in JavaScript, are flagged during compilation. This leads to more reliable and robust code. The use of interfaces and type aliases promotes better design patterns and code organization. Developers can define contracts for objects, ensuring that they adhere to specific structures. This not only enhances code readability but also makes it easier to understand and maintain large codebases.

Another significant advantage is TypeScript's compatibility with existing JavaScript code. TypeScript files can seamlessly integrate with JavaScript files, allowing for a gradual migration of projects from JavaScript to TypeScript. This means teams can start adopting TypeScript incrementally without having to rewrite their entire codebase. TypeScript's support for modern JavaScript features and its ability to compile to JavaScript that runs on any browser or host further enhances its appeal. Developers can write code using the latest ECMAScript features and have it transpiled to work in environments that do not yet support these features natively.

Classic Use-case: Airbnb's Migration to TypeScript

Airbnb, a well-known online marketplace for lodging and tourism experiences, encountered significant issues with its large JavaScript codebase. As the application grew, so did the complexity and number of bugs, many of which were caused by type errors that could only be detected during execution. This resulted in increased maintenance efforts and slower development cycles. To address these issues, Airbnb chose to switch from JavaScript to TypeScript. The migration was motivated by the desire for a more dependable and maintainable codebase. Airbnb intended to use TypeScript's static type checking and enhanced tooling to improve code quality and developer productivity.

Airbnb's migration process was incremental. The team began by converting critical components of the codebase, gradually progressing to full adoption. This approach minimized disruptions and allowed developers to become acquainted with TypeScript while continuing to deliver features and updates. During the transition, Airbnb used TypeScript's interoperability with JavaScript to ensure a smooth and efficient migration process. One of the most notable post-migration benefits was a significant reduction in type-related errors. TypeScript's static typing system identified many issues early in the development process, resulting in fewer bugs reaching production. This improved not only the application's overall stability, but also the developer experience, making debugging and troubleshooting easier and more efficient. Furthermore, the use of TypeScript improved code readability and maintenance. The use of interfaces and type definitions provided clear contracts for data structures, allowing developers to better understand and work with the codebase. This was especially useful for new team members, who were able to ramp up more quickly thanks to the self-documenting nature of TypeScript code. In addition, Airbnb benefited from TypeScript's robust tooling support. IDE features such as intelligent code completion, refactoring tools, and error highlighting have significantly increased developer productivity. These tools allowed developers to write cleaner code faster and with more confidence.

Overall, switching to TypeScript enabled Airbnb to create a more stable, maintainable, and scalable application. The improved code quality and developer experience resulted in shorter development cycles and better user experiences, demonstrating the tangible advantages of using TypeScript in a large-scale production environment.

Setting up TypeScript Environment

Installing TypeScript and Node.js on Windows

To begin working with TypeScript, the first step is to install Node.js, which includes the Node Package Manager (npm) necessary for managing TypeScript installations and other dependencies. Following the given below steps:

- Visit the official Node.js website at www.nodejs.org

- Click on the "LTS" (Long Term Support) version to download the installer suitable for your Windows system.
- Run the downloaded installer.
- Follow the on-screen instructions to complete the installation process.
- Ensure that you check the option to add Node.js to your PATH during the installation process. This allows you to run Node.js and npm commands from the command line.
- Open Command Prompt (you can search for **cmd** in the start menu).
- Type **node -v** and press Enter. This command displays the version of Node.js installed.
- Type **npm -v** and press Enter. This command displays the version of npm installed.

Next, we will install TypeScript using npm:

- In Command Prompt, type **npm install -g typescript** and press Enter.
- The **-g** flag installs TypeScript globally, making the **tsc** (TypeScript compiler) command available from any directory.
- Type **tsc -v** in the Command Prompt and press Enter. This command displays the version of TypeScript installed.

Configuring TypeScript Compiler

With TypeScript installed, the next step is to configure the TypeScript compiler. This involves creating a configuration file that defines the compiler options and settings for your TypeScript project.

Create a Project Directory

- Open Command Prompt and navigate to the directory where you want to create your project. You can use the **cd** command to change directories.
- For example, type **mkdir my-typescript-project** and press Enter to create a new directory. Then, type **cd my-typescript-project** and press Enter to navigate into it.

Initialize a TypeScript Project

- In the project directory, type **tsc --init** and press Enter.
- This command generates a **tsconfig.json** file, which contains the configuration settings for the TypeScript compiler.

Configure tsconfig.json

- Open the **tsconfig.json** file in a text editor. The **tsconfig.json** file includes various options for configuring the TypeScript compiler. The settings include:
    - **target**: Specifies the ECMAScript version to which TypeScript code is compiled (e.g., **es6**, **es2015**, **esnext**).
    - **module**: Defines the module system for the compiled code (e.g., **commonjs**, **es6**).
    - **outDir**: Specifies the output directory for compiled JavaScript files.
    - **rootDir**: Defines the root directory of the TypeScript source files.
    - **strict**: Enables strict type-checking options.

You may check out the following sample configuration:

```
{
  "compilerOptions": {
    "target": "es6",
    "module": "commonjs",
    "outDir": "./dist",
    "rootDir": "./src",
    "strict": true
  }
}
```

- Save the **tsconfig.json** file after making the necessary changes.

Create Source and Output Directories

- In the project directory, create a **src** directory for your TypeScript source files and a **dist** directory for the compiled JavaScript files.
- Type **mkdir src** and **mkdir dist** in the Command Prompt and press Enter.

Compile TypeScript Code

- Create a simple TypeScript file in the **src** directory. For example, create a file named **index.ts** with the following content:

```
const greeting: string = "Hello, TypeScript!";

console.log(greeting);
```

- In the Command Prompt, navigate to the project directory and type **tsc** to compile the TypeScript code. The compiled JavaScript file (**index.js**) will be generated in the **dist** directory.

Installing and Setting up Visual Studio Code

Visual Studio Code (VS Code) is a popular code editor with excellent support for TypeScript development. Follow the below given steps to install and set up VS Code:

Download Visual Studio Code

- Visit the official [Visual Studio Code website](#).
- Click on the "Download for Windows" button to download the installer.
- Run the downloaded installer.
- Follow the on-screen instructions to complete the installation process.
- Ensure that you select the option to add VS Code to your PATH during installation. This allows you to open VS Code from the command line.
- After installation, launch VS Code.
- You can also open VS Code from the command line by typing **code .** in the project directory.
- In VS Code, click on the Extensions icon in the sidebar (or press **Ctrl+Shift+X**).
- Search for "TypeScript" and install the "TypeScript and JavaScript Language Features" extension.

Configure VS Code for TypeScript Development

- Open your TypeScript project in VS Code by navigating to **File > Open Folder** and selecting your project directory.
- VS Code provides built-in support for TypeScript. It automatically recognizes the

- `tsconfig.json` file and uses the TypeScript compiler options defined in it.
- To run your TypeScript code directly from VS Code, open the terminal in VS Code by navigating to **View > Terminal** or pressing **Ctrl+`**.
- In the terminal, type **tsc** to compile the TypeScript code, and then type **node dist/index.js** to run the compiled JavaScript code.

Enable Auto Compilation

- To enable auto-compilation of TypeScript files, you can use the **watch** mode.
- In the terminal, type **tsc -w** to start the TypeScript compiler in watch mode. This automatically recompiles TypeScript files whenever changes are detected.
- You can see the output in the terminal and directly run the updated JavaScript file without manually compiling each time.

Once you've followed these steps, your Windows system will be fully configured for TypeScript development. You've got TypeScript and Node.js installed, the TypeScript compiler configured, and Visual Studio Code set up so that you can develop TypeScript efficiently.

Basic TypeScript Syntax

Variables and Constants

In TypeScript, similar to what in JavaScript, you declare variables using the **let** and **const** keywords. The **let** keyword allows you to declare mutable variables, whereas **const** is used for immutable variables, meaning their values cannot be reassigned once set.

Declaring Variables with let

```
let message: string = "Hello, TypeScript!";
let count: number = 42;
let isAvailable: boolean = true;
```

In the above code, **message** is a string variable, **count** is a number variable, and **isAvailable** is a boolean variable. The colon followed by a type (**: string**, **: number**, **: boolean**) is how TypeScript enforces type annotations.

Declaring Constants with const

```
const pi: number = 3.14;

const welcomeMessage: string = "Welcome to TypeScript!";
```

Here, **pi** and **welcomeMessage** are constants. Their values cannot be changed once assigned. Using **const** ensures that the assigned values remain constant throughout the program.

Data Types

TypeScript offers a range of basic data types that are similar to those in JavaScript but with type annotations to ensure type safety. The commonly used data types include:

Number

All numbers are of type **number**, whether they are integers or floating-point values.

```
let age: number = 25;

let temperature: number = 98.6;
```

String

The **string** type is used for textual data.

```
let firstName: string = "John";

let lastName: string = "Doe";
```

Boolean

The **boolean** type represents true or false values.

```
let isLoggedIn: boolean = false;

let hasPermission: boolean = true;
```

Array

Arrays can hold multiple values of a specific type. They can be declared in two ways.

```
let scores: number[] = [90, 85, 88];
```

```
let names: Array<string> = ["Alice", "Bob", "Charlie"];
```

Tuple

Tuples allow you to store an array with a fixed number of elements, where each element can have a different type.

```
let user: [number, string] = [1, "John Doe"];
```

Enum

Enums provide a way to define a set of named constants.

```
enum Color { Red, Green, Blue }

let c: Color = Color.Green;
```

Any

The **any** type can hold any type of value and is used when the type of a variable is unknown during the development phase.

```
let randomValue: any = 10;

randomValue = "Hello";

randomValue = true;
```

Void

The **void** type is used to represent the absence of a value, commonly used in functions that do not return a value.

```
function logMessage(message: string): void {
    console.log(message);
}
```

Null and Undefined

These types represent the absence of a value. By default, they are subtypes of all other types.

```
let u: undefined = undefined;

let n: null = null;
```

Type Annotations

Type annotations provide a way to explicitly specify the type of a variable, function parameter, or return value. This helps in catching errors early and makes the code more readable and maintainable.

Following is the variable type annotation:

```
let userName: string = "Alice";

let userAge: number = 30;

let isAdmin: boolean = true;
```

And, the function parameter and return type annotations appear like:

```
function greet(name: string): string {
    return `Hello, ${name}!`;
}
```

In this function, **name** is expected to be a string, and the function returns a string.

Comparing TypeScript to JavaScript Syntax

TypeScript is a superset of JavaScript, meaning all valid JavaScript code is also valid TypeScript code. However, TypeScript introduces type annotations and additional features that provide static typing and enhanced development experience.

Variable Declarations

In JavaScript:

```
let message = "Hello, JavaScript!";
```

Whereas, in TypeScript:

```typescript
let message: string = "Hello, TypeScript!";
```

In the TypeScript example, **: string** is added to specify that the **message** must be a string. This type annotation helps catch errors during compilation rather than at runtime.

Function Declarations

In JavaScript:

```javascript
function add(a, b) {
    return a + b;
}
```

Whereas, in TypeScript:

```typescript
function add(a: number, b: number): number {
    return a + b;
}
```

In TypeScript, **a** and **b** are annotated as numbers, and the function is expected to return a number. This ensures that only numbers are passed to the function, preventing runtime errors.

Array Declarations

In JavaScript:

```javascript
let scores = [90, 85, 88];
```

Whereas, in TypeScript:

```typescript
let scores: number[] = [90, 85, 88];
```

In TypeScript, **: number[]** specifies that **scores** is an array of numbers. This type annotation ensures that the array only contains numbers.

Object Declarations

In JavaScript:

```
let person = {
    name: "John",
    age: 30
};
```

Whereas, in TypeScript:

```
let person: { name: string; age: number } = {
    name: "John",
    age: 30
};
```

In TypeScript, **`{ name: string; age: number }`** explicitly defines the structure of the **person** object, specifying that **name** must be a string and **age** must be a number.

Function Parameter and Return Types

In JavaScript, functions do not have type annotations for parameters or return values, which can lead to runtime errors if incorrect types are passed or returned.

Whereas, in TypeScript, function parameters and return values are explicitly typed, providing clear expectations and reducing the risk of errors. For example:

```
function multiply(a: number, b: number): number {
    return a * b;
}
```

In this TypeScript function, **a** and **b** are required to be numbers, and the function returns a number. If non-number values are passed, TypeScript will generate a compile-time error.

Tuples and Enums

JavaScript does not have native support for tuples and enums, which can lead to less structured and harder-to-maintain code when dealing with fixed collections of values or sets of named constants. Whereas, TypeScript introduces tuples and enums to provide more structured and maintainable code. For example:

```
let user: [number, string] = [1, "John Doe"];
enum Status { Active, Inactive, Pending }
let currentStatus: Status = Status.Active;
```

Tuples allow you to define a fixed array of values with specific types, while enums enable the creation of named constants, improving code readability and maintainability.

Type Annotations and Inference

Explicit Type Annotations

TypeScript allows you to explicitly specify the types of variables, function parameters, return values, and object properties. This is known as type annotation. Explicit type annotations help the TypeScript compiler understand the intended data types, reducing errors and improving code readability.

Variable Type Annotations

You can declare the type of a variable explicitly using a colon followed by the type.

```
let username: string = "Alice";
let userAge: number = 30;
let isLoggedIn: boolean = true;
```

In the above code, **username** is explicitly declared as a **string**, **userAge** as a **number**, and **isLoggedIn** as a **boolean**. If you try to assign a value of a different type to these variables, the TypeScript compiler will generate an error.

Function Parameter and Return Type Annotations

You can also specify types for function parameters and return values.

```
function add(a: number, b: number): number {
    return a + b;
```

}
```

In this function, **a** and **b** are explicitly annotated as numbers, and the function returns a number. This ensures that only numbers can be passed to the function and that the function's return value will always be a number.

## Object Type Annotations

When working with objects, you can define the types of properties.

```
let person: { name: string; age: number; isAdmin: boolean } = {
    name: "John",
    age: 25,
    isAdmin: false
};
```

Here, **person** is an object with three properties: **name**, **age**, and **isAdmin**, explicitly annotated as **string**, **number**, and **boolean**, respectively. Any attempt to assign a value of an incorrect type to these properties will result in a compilation error.

Array Type Annotations

Arrays can also be annotated to specify the type of elements they contain.

```
let scores: number[] = [85, 90, 78];
let names: string[] = ["Alice", "Bob", "Charlie"];
```

In these examples, **scores** is an array of numbers, and **names** is an array of strings. The annotations ensure that the arrays only contain elements of the specified types.

Tuple Type Annotations

Tuples allow you to define an array with a fixed number of elements, each with a specific type.

```
let user: [number, string] = [1, "John Doe"];
```
```

In the above code, **user** is a tuple with a number as the first element and a string as the second element. The annotation enforces this structure.

Function Types

You can define the types of functions using a combination of parameter and return type annotations.

```
let multiply: (x: number, y: number) => number = 
function(x: number, y: number): number {

    return x * y;

};
```

In the above code, **multiply** is a function that takes two parameters (**x** and **y**), both of which are numbers, and returns a number. The type annotation ensures that the function adheres to this signature.

Type Inference by Compiler

TypeScript has a powerful type inference system that automatically determines the types of variables and expressions based on the values assigned to them. This can reduce the need for explicit type annotations and make the code more concise.

Variable Type Inference

When you declare a variable and initialize it with a value, TypeScript infers the type from the value.

```
let greeting = "Hello, TypeScript!";

let count = 42;

let isAvailable = true;
```

In the above code, **greeting** is inferred to be a **string**, **count** is inferred to be a **number**, and **isAvailable** is inferred to be a **boolean**. TypeScript infers these types from the assigned values, so there's no need for explicit type annotations.

Function Return Type Inference

TypeScript can also infer the return type of a function based on its return statements.

```typescript
function sum(a: number, b: number) {
    return a + b;
}
```

In this function, TypeScript infers that the return type is **number** because the function returns the sum of two numbers. While explicit return type annotations can enhance code readability and maintainability, they are not always necessary due to TypeScript's inference capabilities.

Complex Type Inference

TypeScript can infer types for more complex structures, such as objects and arrays.

```typescript
let product = {
    id: 1,
    name: "Laptop",
    price: 1000
};
```

In the above code, TypeScript infers that **product** is an object with properties **id** (number), **name** (string), and **price** (number). This inferred type helps ensure that all subsequent operations on the **product** adhere to this structure.

Function Parameter Inference

TypeScript can infer the types of function parameters in certain contexts, such as when a function is used as a callback.

```typescript
let numbers = [1, 2, 3, 4];
numbers.forEach(number => {
    console.log(number);
});
```

In the above code, TypeScript infers that **number** is a **number** because it knows the array

numbers contain numbers. This inference makes the code more concise while maintaining type safety.

Contextual Typing

TypeScript uses the surrounding context to infer types. This is particularly useful in situations like event handlers and callbacks.

```
window.addEventListener("click", (event) => {
    console.log(event.button);
});
```

Here, TypeScript infers that the **event** is of type **MouseEvent** because the **addEventListener** method is known to handle DOM events, specifically mouse events in this case. This inference ensures that the **event** has the properties and methods associated with **MouseEvent**.

Combining Type Annotations and Inference

You can combine explicit type annotations and inference for greater clarity and flexibility.

```
function displayUserInfo(name: string, age: number) {
    let message = `User ${name} is ${age} years old.`;
    console.log(message);
}
```

In this function, the parameters **name** and **age** are explicitly annotated, but the variable **message** is inferred to be a **string** based on its initialization. This approach leverages the strengths of both explicit annotations and inference.

Inferred Types in Arrays and Objects

When dealing with arrays and objects, TypeScript infers the types of elements or properties based on the values assigned.

```
let colors = ["red", "green", "blue"];
let user = {
```

```
    id: 1,
    name: "Alice"
};
```

In these examples, **colors** is inferred to be an array of strings, and **user** is inferred to be an object with **id** as a number and **name** as a string. TypeScript's type inference ensures that operations on these variables remain type-safe.

Function Type Inference with Higher-Order Functions

TypeScript can infer the types of parameters and return values in higher-order functions.

```
function createArray<T>(length: number, value: T): T[] {
    return Array(length).fill(value);
}


let stringArray = createArray(3, "hello");
let numberArray = createArray(3, 42);
```

In the above code, TypeScript infers that **stringArray** is a **string[]** and **numberArray** is a **number[]** based on the arguments passed to **createArray**. The generic type **T** is inferred from the context, making the function versatile and type-safe.

Compiling TypeScript to JavaScript

What is Compilation?

Compilation is the process of translating source code written in a high-level programming language into a lower-level language, such as machine code or an intermediate language that can be executed by a computer. In the context of TypeScript, compilation refers to converting TypeScript code into JavaScript, the language that browsers and other JavaScript engines can understand and execute.

TypeScript is a statically typed superset of JavaScript, which means it introduces additional syntax and features on top of standard JavaScript. However, web browsers and most JavaScript environments do not natively support TypeScript. Therefore, TypeScript code must be compiled into JavaScript before it can be run.

The Compilation Process

The TypeScript compilation process involves several steps:

1. **Parsing**: The TypeScript compiler (tsc) reads the TypeScript code and parses it into an abstract syntax tree (AST), which represents the structure of the code.

2. **Type Checking**: The compiler checks the code for type errors based on the type annotations and type inference. It ensures that the types of variables, function parameters, return values, and object properties are consistent and correct.

3. **Transpilation**: The TypeScript code is transpiled into JavaScript. During this step, the TypeScript-specific syntax is converted into standard JavaScript syntax.

4. **Emitting**: The compiler generates the final JavaScript output files from the transpiled code. These files can then be executed in any JavaScript environment.

This process ensures that TypeScript code is type-safe and error-free before being transformed into JavaScript.

'tsc' Command

The **tsc** (TypeScript Compiler) command is used to compile TypeScript code into JavaScript. It is a powerful tool that allows you to compile single files or entire projects with ease. To use the **tsc** command, you need to have TypeScript installed on your system.

Now, to compile a single TypeScript file, use the following command:

```
tsc filename.ts
```

This command compiles **filename.ts** into a corresponding JavaScript file, **filename.js**, in the same directory.

If you have multiple TypeScript files to compile, you can list them all in the command:

```
tsc file1.ts file2.ts file3.ts
```

For larger projects, it's more efficient to use a configuration file (**tsconfig.json**). This file defines the project's compilation settings and includes all the files to be compiled. To compile a project with a **tsconfig.json** file, simply run:

```
tsc
```

This command reads the configuration from **tsconfig.json** and compiles the entire project according to the specified settings.

Configuring tsconfig.json

The **tsconfig.json** file is a configuration file that specifies the TypeScript compiler options and the files to be included in the project. It allows you to customize the compilation process and manage project settings in a centralized way.

Creating tsconfig.json

To create a **tsconfig.json** file, navigate to your project directory in the command line and run:

```
tsc --init
```

This command generates a default **tsconfig.json** file with a basic configuration.

Understanding tsconfig.json

The **tsconfig.json** file contains several key sections:

- **compilerOptions**: This section defines the compiler options and settings.
- **include**: Specifies the files or directories to be included in the compilation process.
- **exclude**: Specifies the files or directories to be excluded from the compilation process.
- **files**: Lists the specific files to be compiled.

Configuring compilerOptions

The **compilerOptions** section allows you to customize various aspects of the compilation process. Given below are some common options:

- **target**: Specifies the ECMAScript version to which the TypeScript code should be compiled. Examples include es5, es6, es2015, and esnext.
- **module**: Defines the module system for the compiled code. Examples include commonjs, es6, and amd.
- **outDir**: Specifies the output directory for the compiled JavaScript files.

- **rootDir**: Defines the root directory of the TypeScript source files.
- **strict**: Enables strict type-checking options.
- **sourceMap**: Generates source maps for easier debugging.

Following is the sample `tsconfig.json` configuration:

```
{
  "compilerOptions": {
    "target": "es6",
    "module": "commonjs",
    "outDir": "./dist",
    "rootDir": "./src",
    "strict": true,
    "sourceMap": true
  },
  "include": ["src/**/*.ts"],
  "exclude": ["node_modules"]
}
```

With the `tsconfig.json` file configured, you can compile your project by running the `tsc` command in the project directory. The compiled JavaScript files are output to the directory specified in the `outDir` option.

Project Structure

Given below is an example of a simple project structure:

```
my-typescript-project/
├── src/
```

```
|   ├── index.ts
|   └── utils.ts
├── dist/
└── tsconfig.json
```

Here, in this project, the **src** directory contains the TypeScript source files, and the **dist** directory is the output directory for the compiled JavaScript files. The **tsconfig.json** file is located in the root of the project.

Compiling the Project

In the **src/index.ts** file, you might have the following TypeScript code:

```
import { greet } from "./utils";


const message: string = greet("TypeScript");
console.log(message);
```

In the **src/utils.ts** file, you might have:

```
export function greet(name: string): string {
    return `Hello, ${name}!`;
}
```

By understanding the compilation process, using the **tsc** command, and configuring the **tsconfig.json** file, you can effectively manage and compile your TypeScript projects. This setup ensures that your TypeScript code is correctly transformed into JavaScript, ready to be executed in any JavaScript environment.

Summary

Beginning with a brief outline of TypeScript's background and development, this chapter dove headfirst into the language's essentials. We learned about TypeScript's key features and benefits, including improved code quality, a better developer experience, and early error detection. We also looked at a real-world example of Airbnb migrating from JavaScript to TypeScript, which demonstrated the tangible benefits of using TypeScript in a large-scale production environment.

We then learned how to set up the TypeScript environment on a Windows system, which included installing Node.js and TypeScript, configuring the TypeScript compiler, and configuring Visual Studio Code to facilitate TypeScript development. We covered TypeScript's basic syntax, which includes variables, constants, data types, and type annotations, as well as compared TypeScript syntax to JavaScript syntax to demonstrate the additional structure and type safety it provides. We then looked at type annotations and inference, including how to explicitly specify types for variables, function parameters, return values, and object properties, as well as how TypeScript's powerful type inference system determines types based on assigned values.

Finally, we looked at how to compile TypeScript to JavaScript, which included learning about the tsc command and configuring the tsconfig.json file to manage compilation settings and streamline development. In sum, this chapter established foundations for future chapters' more advanced material and practical applications by providing a firm grasp of TypeScript and how to work with it.

Chapter 2: Working with Basic Types

Chapter Overview

Building strong and type-safe applications relies on a solid understanding of TypeScript's core data types, which are the focus of this chapter. We begin by looking at the fundamental types: numbers, strings, and booleans. Understanding these basic types matters because they serve as the foundation for any TypeScript program, allowing you to effectively work with numerical data, textual information, and boolean logic.

Next, we will look at arrays and tuples. Arrays allow you to store multiple values of the same type, whereas tuples can store a fixed number of elements of different types. Mastering these data structures will improve your ability to manage and use large amounts of data in your applications. We will look at how TypeScript's type system outperforms JavaScript in terms of safety and structure. Following that, we will look at enum types, which allow you to define a set of named constants. Enums improve code readability and maintainability by assigning meaningful names to sets of related values. We will look at how to define and use enums, making your code more intuitive and manageable.

Finally, we will learn more advanced types like any, unknown, void, null, and undefined. These types are useful in situations where greater flexibility is required or when the absence of a value must be represented. Understanding how to use these types properly allows you to handle a variety of edge cases while also ensuring that your TypeScript code is robust and versatile. This chapter aims to give you a thorough understanding of these fundamental types, allowing you to create more reliable and maintainable TypeScript applications.

Number, String, and Boolean Types

From this chapter onwards, we will learn all the concepts of TypeScript through a live interactive project called "Anna's TS Coaching" and will continue using it throughout our book in order to have a very effective and practical learning experience. In this section, we will start by incorporating fundamental TypeScript data types: number, string, and boolean. These types will help us manage numerical data, textual information, and boolean logic, which are essential for any application.

Declaring Number Variables

First, let's declare some number variables to represent different numerical values in our project. Suppose Anna's TS Coaching wants to track the number of students enrolled, the average score of students, and the maximum capacity of the coaching center.

Creating the Project Directory

Open your terminal and create a new directory for the project, then navigate into it:

```
mkdir annas-ts-coaching

cd annas-ts-coaching
```

Initializing the Project

Initialize the project by creating a **tsconfig.json** file:

```
tsc --init
```

Creating Source Files

Create a source directory and a TypeScript file:

```
mkdir src

cd src

touch index.ts
```

Declaring Number Variables

Open **index.ts** in your preferred text editor and declare the number variables:

```typescript
// Number variables for Anna's TS Coaching

let studentsEnrolled: number = 30;

let averageScore: number = 85.5;

let maxCapacity: number = 50;


console.log(`Students Enrolled: ${studentsEnrolled}`);

console.log(`Average Score: ${averageScore}`);

console.log(`Maximum Capacity: ${maxCapacity}`);
```

In the above code, **studentsEnrolled**, **averageScore**, and **maxCapacity** are declared as numbers. We use **`console.log`** to print these values to the console.

Compiling and Running the Code

Compile the TypeScript code to JavaScript and run the compiled JavaScript file:

```
tsc
```

```
node dist/index.js
```

Using Strings

Next, we will work with string variables to manage textual information such as the names of courses and instructors.

Declaring String Variables

Add the following code to **`index.ts`**:

```
// String variables for Anna's TS Coaching
let courseName: string = "TypeScript Basics";
let instructorName: string = "Anna";


console.log(`Course Name: ${courseName}`);
console.log(`Instructor Name: ${instructorName}`);
```

Here, **`courseName`** and **`instructorName`** are declared as strings, representing the name of the course and the instructor.

Concatenating Strings

You can concatenate strings using template literals:

```
let welcomeMessage: string = `Welcome to ${courseName} by ${instructorName}!`;
```

```
console.log(welcomeMessage);
```

The template literals make it easy to include variables within strings. And, then compile and run the code to see the output.

Constructing Boolean Logics and Conditions

Boolean variables help manage true/false values and can be used to control the flow of your application using conditional statements.

Declaring Boolean Variables

Add the following boolean variables to **index.ts**:

```
// Boolean variables for Anna's TS Coaching

let isEnrollmentOpen: boolean = true;

let hasVacancies: boolean = studentsEnrolled < maxCapacity;


console.log(`Is Enrollment Open? ${isEnrollmentOpen}`);

console.log(`Has Vacancies? ${hasVacancies}`);
```

In the above code, **isEnrollmentOpen** indicates if enrollment is open, and **hasVacancies** checks if the number of students enrolled is less than the maximum capacity.

Using Boolean Logic in Conditions

You can use boolean variables in conditional statements to control program flow:

```
// Conditional logic based on boolean variables

if (isEnrollmentOpen && hasVacancies) {

    console.log("Students can enroll in the course.");

} else if (!hasVacancies) {

    console.log("The course is full.");
```

```typescript
} else {
    console.log("Enrollment is currently closed.");
}
```

This above code checks if enrollment is open and if there are vacancies, then prints appropriate messages.

Arrays and Tuples

In this section, we will extend our project by exploring arrays and tuples, which are essential data structures for managing collections of data in TypeScript.

Declaring and Initializing Arrays

Arrays are used to store multiple values of the same type. We will start by declaring and initializing arrays to keep track of student names and their respective scores.

Declaring Arrays

Arrays can be declared using the **Array** generic type or the shorthand syntax with square brackets (**[]**).

```typescript
// Using Array generic type
let studentNames: Array<string> = ["Alice", "Bob", "Charlie"];
let studentScores: Array<number> = [85, 92, 78];


// Using shorthand syntax
let courseTitles: string[] = ["TypeScript Basics", "Advanced TypeScript"];
let courseDurations: number[] = [10, 15];
```

Here, **studentNames** and **courseTitles** are arrays of strings, while **studentScores** and **courseDurations** are arrays of numbers.

Initializing Arrays

Arrays can be initialized with values directly or using the **Array** constructor.

```
let newStudentNames: string[] = [];
let newStudentScores: number[] = new Array(3);


// Adding values to the arrays
newStudentNames.push("Dave", "Eve");
newStudentScores[0] = 88;
newStudentScores[1] = 76;
newStudentScores[2] = 90;


console.log(newStudentNames);
console.log(newStudentScores);
```

In the above code, **newStudentNames** is initialized as an empty array, and **newStudentScores** is initialized with a specified length.

Using Tuples

Tuples are a special type of array where the types of elements are known and can be different. Tuples are useful for representing structured data.

Declaring Tuples

We will declare tuples to store student information, such as their name and score.

```
let studentInfo: [string, number];
```

```
// Initializing the tuple
studentInfo = ["Alice", 85];

console.log(`Student Name: ${studentInfo[0]}`);
console.log(`Student Score: ${studentInfo[1]}`);
```

In the above code, **studentInfo** is a tuple with a string (name) and a number (score).

Using Tuple Types

Tuples can also be used with more complex structures. For example, we can store multiple pieces of information for each course.

```
let courseDetails: [string, number, boolean];

// Initializing the tuple
courseDetails = ["TypeScript Basics", 10, true];

console.log(`Course Title: ${courseDetails[0]}`);
console.log(`Course Duration: ${courseDetails[1]} hours`);
console.log(`Course Active: ${courseDetails[2]}`);
```

Here, **courseDetails** is a tuple with a string (course title), a number (duration in hours), and a boolean (whether the course is active).

Nested Tuples

Tuples can be nested to represent more complex data structures.

```
let nestedTuple: [number, [string, boolean]];
```

```
// Initializing the nested tuple
nestedTuple = [1, ["Introduction to TypeScript", true]];

console.log(`Course ID: ${nestedTuple[0]}`);
console.log(`Course Name: ${nestedTuple[1][0]}`);
console.log(`Course Active: ${nestedTuple[1][1]}`);
```

In the above code, **nestedTuple** contains a number and another tuple.

Array Methods and Operations

TypeScript arrays come with several built-in methods that make it easy to manipulate and interact with the data. We will explore some common array methods and operations.

Adding and Removing Elements

Use **push** to add elements to the end of an array and **pop** to remove the last element.

```
let students: string[] = ["Alice", "Bob", "Charlie"];


// Adding elements
students.push("Dave");
console.log(students); // ["Alice", "Bob", "Charlie", "Dave"]


// Removing the last element
let lastStudent = students.pop();
```

```typescript
console.log(students); // ["Alice", "Bob", "Charlie"]
console.log(`Removed Student: ${lastStudent}`);
```

Finding Elements

Use **indexOf** to find the index of an element and **includes** to check if an element exists in the array.

```typescript
let scores: number[] = [85, 92, 78, 88, 76];


// Finding the index of an element
let index = scores.indexOf(88);
console.log(`Index of 88: ${index}`); // 3


// Checking if an element exists
let hasHighScore = scores.includes(92);
console.log(`Has High Score: ${hasHighScore}`); // true
```

Iterating Over Arrays

Use **forEach** to iterate over the elements of an array.

```typescript
let courseTitles: string[] = ["TypeScript Basics", "Advanced TypeScript"];


// Iterating over the array
courseTitles.forEach((title, index) => {
    console.log(`Course ${index + 1}: ${title}`);
```

});

Transforming Arrays

Use **map** to transform the elements of an array.

```
let scores: number[] = [85, 92, 78, 88, 76];


// Transforming the array
let adjustedScores = scores.map(score => score + 5);
console.log(adjustedScores); // [90, 97, 83, 93, 81]
```

Filtering Arrays

Use **filter** to create a new array with elements that meet certain criteria.

```
let scores: number[] = [85, 92, 78, 88, 76];


// Filtering the array
let highScores = scores.filter(score => score >= 85);
console.log(highScores); // [85, 92, 88]
```

Reducing Arrays

Use **reduce** to reduce the array to a single value.

```
let scores: number[] = [85, 92, 78, 88, 76];


// Reducing the array
let totalScore = scores.reduce((total, score) => total + score, 0);
```

```
console.log(`Total Score: ${totalScore}`); // 419
```

Throughout this topic, we declared and initialized arrays to manage collections of data such as student names, grades, and course information. We experimented with different array methods and operations, such as adding and removing elements, finding elements, iterating over arrays, transforming arrays, filtering arrays, and reducing them. We also learned about tuples, which allow us to store structured data of various types.

Enum Types

Enums, short for enumerations, are a feature that allows you to define a set of named constants. Enums make your code more readable and maintainable by providing meaningful names for sets of related values. Enums are a way of giving more friendly names to sets of numeric or string values. They are useful for representing a fixed set of related constants, such as days of the week, status codes, or categories. In TypeScript, enums can be numeric or string-based.

Defining Enums

We will define an enum to represent different levels of courses offered by Anna's TS Coaching. We will define an enum called **CourseLevel** with three levels: Beginner, Intermediate, and Advanced.

Defining Numeric Enums

Numeric enums are the default in TypeScript. The enum members are assigned numeric values starting from 0.

```
// Defining a numeric enum for course levels
enum CourseLevel {
    Beginner,
    Intermediate,
    Advanced
}


// Using the enum
```

```typescript
let courseLevel: CourseLevel = CourseLevel.Beginner;

console.log(`Course Level: ${CourseLevel[courseLevel]}`);
// Output: Course Level: Beginner
```

In the above code, **CourseLevel** is a numeric enum with members **Beginner**, **Intermediate**, and **Advanced**. The **CourseLevel[courseLevel]** syntax is used to get the name of the enum member.

Defining String Enums

String enums allow you to explicitly assign string values to the enum members.

```typescript
// Defining a string enum for course levels
enum CourseLevel {
    Beginner = "BEGINNER",
    Intermediate = "INTERMEDIATE",
    Advanced = "ADVANCED"
}


// Using the enum
let courseLevel: CourseLevel = CourseLevel.Beginner;

console.log(`Course Level: ${courseLevel}`); // Output: Course Level: BEGINNER
```

In the above code, **CourseLevel** is a string enum with members assigned specific string values. The output directly shows the string value of the enum member.

Enum Members and Values

Enum members can be accessed using both their names and values. We will explore how to work with enum members and values in our ongoing project.

Accessing Enum Members

You can access enum members using the dot notation and retrieve their values.

```
// Accessing enum members
let beginnerLevel: CourseLevel = CourseLevel.Beginner;
let intermediateLevel: CourseLevel = CourseLevel.Intermediate;
let advancedLevel: CourseLevel = CourseLevel.Advanced;

console.log(beginnerLevel); // Output: BEGINNER
console.log(intermediateLevel); // Output: INTERMEDIATE
console.log(advancedLevel); // Output: ADVANCED
```

The above code snippet demonstrates how to assign enum members to variables and print their values.

Using Enums in Functions

Enums can be used as function parameters to ensure that only valid enum values are passed.

```
// Function using enum as a parameter
function getCourseDetails(level: CourseLevel): void {
    switch(level) {
        case CourseLevel.Beginner:
            console.log("Course Level: Beginner - Suitable for newcomers.");
            break;
        case CourseLevel.Intermediate:
```

```
            console.log("Course Level: Intermediate - For those with basic knowledge.");

            break;

        case CourseLevel.Advanced:

            console.log("Course Level: Advanced - For experienced learners.");

            break;

    }

}


// Calling the function with different enum values

getCourseDetails(CourseLevel.Beginner);

getCourseDetails(CourseLevel.Intermediate);

getCourseDetails(CourseLevel.Advanced);
```

The above code snippet shows how to use enums in a function to control the flow based on the enum values. The **switch** statement checks the enum value and prints the corresponding message.

Reverse Mapping of Numeric Enums

Numeric enums support reverse mapping, which means you can get the name of an enum member using its value.

```
// Defining a numeric enum for days of the week

enum DaysOfWeek {

    Sunday,

    Monday,
```

```
    Tuesday,
    Wednesday,
    Thursday,
    Friday,
    Saturday
}
```

```
// Accessing enum member by value
let day: DaysOfWeek = DaysOfWeek.Wednesday;
console.log(`Day: ${DaysOfWeek[day]}`); // Output: Day: Wednesday
```

In the above code, **DaysOfWeek** is a numeric enum, and **DaysOfWeek[day]** retrieves the name of the enum member. Overall, this provided a strong understanding of enums and how these enums enhance the readability and maintainability of typescript codes.

Any, Unknown, and Void Types

Now, we move to three important types in TypeScrip i.e. **any**, **unknown**, and **void**. These types are used in specific scenarios where type flexibility or the absence of a value is required. Understanding these types will help you handle various situations more effectively.

'any' Type

The **any** type is a flexible type that allows you to assign any value to a variable. It bypasses TypeScript's type-checking system, meaning any operations can be performed on it without raising compile-time errors. This type is useful when migrating JavaScript code to TypeScript or when you need a placeholder type.

```
let anyValue: any = 42;
anyValue = "Hello";
```

```
anyValue = true;
```

In the above code, **anyValue** can hold values of different types: a number, a string, or a boolean. However, using the **any** type reduces the benefits of TypeScript's type-checking, so it should be used sparingly.

'unknown' Type

The **unknown** type is similar to **any**, but it is safer and more restrictive. It requires type-checking before performing operations on variables of this type. It is useful when the type of a variable is not known initially, and you want to perform type-checking at runtime.

```
let unknownValue: unknown = 42;

unknownValue = "Hello";


if (typeof unknownValue === "string") {

    console.log(unknownValue.toUpperCase()); // Safe to use string methods

}
```

In the above code, **unknownValue** can hold values of different types, but type-checking is required before using it as a specific type.

'void' Type

The **void** type represents the absence of a value and is commonly used in functions that do not return a value. It indicates that a function performs a side effect but does not return any data.

```
function logMessage(message: string): void {

    console.log(message);

}
```

In the above code, the **logMessage** function has a return type of **void**, indicating that it does not return any value.

Sample Program

We will incorporate these types into our project to understand their practical applications.

Using 'any' Type

Suppose we need a variable to temporarily store any type of data coming from various sources, such as user inputs or API responses, where the exact type is not known.

```
// Using the any type

let inputData: any;


inputData = "Alice";

console.log(`Name: ${inputData}`);


inputData = 25;

console.log(`Age: ${inputData}`);


inputData = { enrolled: true, course: "TypeScript Basics" };

console.log(`Enrollment Data: ${JSON.stringify(inputData)}`);
```

In the above code, **inputData** can hold a string, a number, or an object. While **any** allows flexibility, it bypasses type safety, so use it with caution.

Using 'unknown' Type

To improve type safety, we can use the **unknown** type when handling data whose type is initially unknown but needs type-checking before use.

```
// Using the unknown type
```

```
let userResponse: unknown;

userResponse = "Accepted";

if (typeof userResponse === "string") {
    console.log(`Response: ${userResponse.toUpperCase()}`);
}

userResponse = { accepted: true, date: "2024-08-01" };

if (typeof userResponse === "object" && userResponse !== null) {
    console.log(`Response Data: ${JSON.stringify(userResponse)}`);
}
```

In the above code, **userResponse** can hold different types, but type-checking ensures safe usage.

Using 'void' Type

In our project, we can use the **void** type for functions that perform actions but do not return values, such as logging or sending notifications.

```
// Using the void type

function notifyUser(message: string): void {
    console.log(`Notification: ${message}`);
```

```
}
```

```
notifyUser("New course available: Advanced TypeScript");
```

In the above code, the **notifyUser** function has a **void** return type, indicating it performs an action without returning a value.

Null and Undefined

Now, we will explore how to work with **null** and **undefined** values. These values represent the absence of data and are important concepts to understand for effective error handling and safe coding practices. We will also delve into type guards, optional chaining, and nullish coalescing to manage these values more efficiently in our project.

Managing Null and Undefined Values

In both JavaScript and TypeScript, **null** and **undefined** are used to represent missing or uninitialized values.

- **undefined**: A variable that has been declared but not assigned a value.
- **null**: A variable explicitly assigned null indicates the intentional absence of any object value.

We will see how these values can be used in our project.

```
// Declaring variables with null and undefined

let studentName: string | null = null;

let studentScore: number | undefined = undefined;


console.log(`Student Name: ${studentName}`); // Output: Student Name: null

console.log(`Student Score: ${studentScore}`); // Output: Student Score: undefined
```

In the above code, **studentName** is explicitly set to **null**, and **studentScore** is set to **undefined**. The use of union types (**string | null** and **number | undefined**) allows these variables to accept multiple types.

You can also assign values to variables that were initially **null** or **undefined**.

```
// Assigning values later
studentName = "Alice";
studentScore = 85;

console.log(`Student Name: ${studentName}`); // Output: Student Name: Alice
console.log(`Student Score: ${studentScore}`); // Output: Student Score: 85
```

Here, **studentName** and **studentScore** are updated with valid values after their initial declaration.

Exploring Type Guards

Type guards are a way to check the type of a variable before performing operations on it. They are particularly useful when dealing with **null** and **undefined** values.

Using Type Guards

Type guards can be implemented using **typeof**, **instanceof**, and other checks.

```
// Function to print student details with type guards
function printStudentDetails(name: string | null, score: number | undefined): void {
    if (name !== null) {
        console.log(`Student Name: ${name}`);
    } else {
```

```
        console.log("Student Name is not available.");
    }

    if (typeof score === "number") {
        console.log(`Student Score: ${score}`);
    } else {
        console.log("Student Score is not available.");
    }
}


// Calling the function
printStudentDetails(studentName, studentScore);
```

In the above code, type guards are used to safely check whether **name** and **score** are available before printing their values.

Understanding Optional Chaining and Nullish Coalescing

Optional chaining and nullish coalescing are powerful features that help you safely access properties and provide default values when dealing with **null** or **undefined**.

Optional Chaining

Optional chaining (**?.**) allows you to safely access nested properties of an object without throwing an error if a property is **null** or **undefined**.

```
// Example object
let course: { title?: string; duration?: number } = { title: "TypeScript Basics" };
```

```typescript
// Using optional chaining
console.log(`Course Title: ${course?.title}`); // Output: Course Title: TypeScript Basics
console.log(`Course Duration: ${course?.duration}`); // Output: Course Duration: undefined
```

In the above code, optional chaining is used to access **title** and **duration** properties of the **course** object. If a property is **undefined**, it simply returns **undefined** instead of throwing an error.

Nullish Coalescing

Nullish coalescing (**??**) provides a way to set a default value when a variable is **null** or **undefined**.

```typescript
// Using nullish coalescing
let courseDuration: number = course.duration ?? 10;
console.log(`Course Duration: ${courseDuration}`); // Output: Course Duration: 10
```

In the above code, **courseDuration** is set to the value of **course.duration** if it is not **null** or **undefined**. Otherwise, it defaults to **10**.

Using Optional Chaining and Nullish Coalescing in Functions

We will see how these features can be used in a function to handle optional properties.

```typescript
// Function to get course details with optional chaining and nullish coalescing
function getCourseDetails(course: { title?: string; duration?: number }): void {
    let title = course?.title ?? "Untitled Course";
```

```
    let duration = course?.duration ?? 0;

    console.log(`Course Title: ${title}`);
    console.log(`Course Duration: ${duration} hours`);
}

// Calling the function
getCourseDetails(course);
getCourseDetails({}); // Passing an empty object
```

In this function, optional chaining is used to access the **title** and **duration** properties safely, and nullish coalescing provides default values when these properties are missing.

Summary

This chapter covered the basics of TypeScript data types and structures, starting with strings, booleans, and numbers. We learned how to declare and initialize number variables to represent numerical data, as well as how to manage textual information by concatenating strings with template literals. Booleans were used to create logic and conditions, which allowed us to control program flow through conditional statements. We then looked at arrays and tuples, learning how arrays store collections of values of the same type, whereas tuples allow for fixed collections of different types. We learned various array methods, such as adding, removing, filtering, and transforming elements.

The chapter also covered enum types, which use named constants to improve code readability and maintainability. We created numeric and string enums and used them to represent course levels in our project. Furthermore, we learned the any, unknown, and void types. The any type provided flexibility by bypassing type-checking, whereas the unknown type required type-checking for safe operation. The void type was used for functions that did not return a value, indicating that they performed an action instead.

Finally, we looked at how to handle null and undefined values with union types and type guards to ensure safe operations. We looked at optional chaining and nullish coalescing, which are mechanisms for safely accessing nested properties and setting default values, respectively. These features helped to prevent runtime errors and improve the robustness of our project. This chapter provided us with the fundamental knowledge required to effectively work with TypeScript's basic types, laying the groundwork for more complex concepts in subsequent chapters.

Chapter 3: Functions in TypeScript

Chapter Overview

In this chapter, we will look at TypeScript functions, which are an essential part of developing applications. Functions allow us to encapsulate logic, resulting in code that is reusable and modular. We start by looking at function types and signatures, which define the parameters and return types in our programs. This ensures type safety and consistency. Understanding function types will help us create precise and dependable functions for our project.

Next, we will look at optional and default parameters, which help functions handle different input scenarios gracefully. Optional parameters enable arguments to be omitted, whereas default parameters provide fallback values. We will then look at rest parameters and overloads, which allow functions to handle an infinite number of arguments and provide multiple signatures for various input types, respectively. These features enable us to design functions that are flexible and versatile, meeting a wide range of needs.

The chapter also teaches arrow functions and their impact on **this** context, which is a common source of confusion in JavaScript. Arrow functions have a more concise syntax and provide a consistent context, which can be especially useful in certain programming patterns. Finally, we will look at callback functions and higher-order functions, which let us pass functions as arguments and return them from other functions. These concepts are critical when working with asynchronous code and functional programming patterns. Throughout this chapter, we will apply these concepts to our project, enhancing its functionality and demonstrating the power and flexibility of TypeScript's function capabilities.

Function Types and Signatures

Functions can be categorized based on their declaration, signature, and return type. We will cover regular functions, function expressions, and arrow functions, and also learn about function signatures and call signatures and how they are used to ensure type safety in our code.

Regular Functions

Regular functions are similar to those in JavaScript, but with added type annotations for parameters and return values.

```
// Regular function to calculate student grades

function calculateGrade(score: number): string {
    if (score >= 90) {
        return "A";
```

```
    } else if (score >= 80) {
        return "B";
    } else if (score >= 70) {
        return "C";
    } else if (score >= 60) {
        return "D";
    } else {
        return "F";
    }
}


// Using the regular function
const studentScore = 85;
const studentGrade = calculateGrade(studentScore);
console.log(`Student Score: ${studentScore}, Grade: ${studentGrade}`);
```

In the above code, **calculateGrade** is a regular function that takes a **number** as a parameter and returns a **string**. The function evaluates the score and assigns a grade based on the provided logic.

Function Expressions

Function expressions allow functions to be assigned to variables. This makes them more flexible as they can be used as first-class citizens.

```
// Function expression to greet a student
```

```typescript
const greetStudent = function(name: string): string {
    return `Hello, ${name}! Welcome to Anna's TS Coaching.`;
};



// Using the function expression
const greetingMessage = greetStudent("Alice");
console.log(greetingMessage);
```

In the above code, **greetStudent** is a function expression assigned to a constant variable. It takes a **string** as a parameter and returns a greeting message.

Arrow Functions

Arrow functions provide a concise syntax for writing functions and automatically bind **this** context.

```typescript
// Arrow function to calculate course duration in weeks
const calculateCourseDuration = (hoursPerDay: number, totalHours: number): number => {
    return Math.ceil(totalHours / (hoursPerDay * 5)); // Assuming 5 days a week
};


// Using the arrow function
const courseDuration = calculateCourseDuration(2, 40);
console.log(`Course Duration: ${courseDuration} weeks`);
```

In the above code, **calculateCourseDuration** is an arrow function that calculates the course duration in weeks based on the number of hours per day and the total course hours.

Function Signatures and Call Signatures

Function signatures, also known as call signatures, define the structure of a function by specifying the types of its parameters and return value. They allow TypeScript to enforce type-checking and ensure that functions are called with the correct arguments.

Understanding Function Signatures

Function signatures provide a way to define the expected input and output of a function, helping to maintain type safety. A function signature specifies the number of parameters, their types, and the return type of the function.

```typescript
// Function signature for a calculation function
type CalculationFunction = (a: number, b: number) => number;


// Implementing a function using the signature
const add: CalculationFunction = (a, b) => a + b;
const subtract: CalculationFunction = (a, b) => a - b;


// Using the functions
console.log(`Add: ${add(5, 3)}`); // Output: Add: 8
console.log(`Subtract: ${subtract(5, 3)}`); // Output: Subtract: 2
```

In the above code, **CalculationFunction** is a function signature that defines a function taking two **number** parameters and returning a **number**. The **add** and **subtract** functions are implemented using this signature, ensuring type safety.

We will see how function signatures can be used in our project to define operations such as calculating scores and providing feedback.

```typescript
// Function signature for score calculation
type ScoreCalculator = (scores: number[]) => number;

// Implementing a function using the signature
const averageScore: ScoreCalculator = (scores) => {
    const total = scores.reduce((sum, score) => sum + score, 0);
    return total / scores.length;
};

// Using the function
const scores = [85, 90, 78, 92];
const avgScore = averageScore(scores);
console.log(`Average Score: ${avgScore}`); // Output: Average Score: 86.25
```

In the above code, **ScoreCalculator** is a function signature that defines a function taking an array of **number** and returning a **number**. The **averageScore** function calculates the average score of the students.

Call Signatures in Object Types

Call signatures can also be used within object types to define methods for an object.

```typescript
// Defining an object with a call signature
type CourseDetails = {
    title: string;
```

```
    calculateDuration: (hoursPerDay: number, totalHours:
number) => number;
};


// Implementing the object
const course: CourseDetails = {
    title: "Advanced TypeScript",
    calculateDuration: (hoursPerDay, totalHours) =>
Math.ceil(totalHours / (hoursPerDay * 5))
};


// Using the method
const duration = course.calculateDuration(2, 60);
console.log(`Course: ${course.title}, Duration:
${duration} weeks`);
```

In the above code, **CourseDetails** is an object type with a call signature for the **calculateDuration** method. The **course** object implements this method, allowing us to calculate the duration of the course based on the specified parameters.

Optional and Default Parameters

Optional Parameters

Optional parameters are parameters that may or may not be provided when calling a function. In TypeScript, optional parameters are defined by adding a question mark (**?**) after the parameter name in the function signature. This indicates that the parameter is optional and can be omitted when the function is invoked.

We will define a function in our project that calculates the total score of a student, optionally including bonus points if they exist.

```
// Function to calculate total score with optional bonus
function calculateTotalScore(score: number, bonus?: number): number {
    // If bonus is provided, add it to the score, otherwise return the score
    return score + (bonus || 0);
}


// Using the function with and without bonus points
const totalScore1 = calculateTotalScore(85);
const totalScore2 = calculateTotalScore(85, 10);


console.log(`Total Score without Bonus: ${totalScore1}`);
// Output: Total Score without Bonus: 85

console.log(`Total Score with Bonus: ${totalScore2}`);
// Output: Total Score with Bonus: 95
```

In the above code, the **calculateTotalScore** function has an optional parameter **bonus**. If **bonus** is not provided, it defaults to **0**. The function is called twice, once with a bonus and once without, demonstrating how optional parameters can be omitted.

Default Parameter Values

Default parameter values allow functions to use a default value for a parameter if no argument is provided for it. This simplifies function calls and reduces the need for additional logic to handle missing parameters.

We will update the previous function to use a default value for the bonus parameter.

```typescript
// Function to calculate total score with default bonus value
function calculateTotalScoreWithDefault(score: number, bonus: number = 5): number {
    // Add bonus to the score, using default value if bonus is not provided
    return score + bonus;
}


// Using the function with and without specifying bonus points
const totalScore3 = calculateTotalScoreWithDefault(85);
const totalScore4 = calculateTotalScoreWithDefault(85, 10);


console.log(`Total Score with Default Bonus: ${totalScore3}`); // Output: Total Score with Default Bonus: 90
console.log(`Total Score with Custom Bonus: ${totalScore4}`);  // Output: Total Score with Custom Bonus: 95
```

In the above code, the **calculateTotalScoreWithDefault** function has a default value of **5** for the **bonus** parameter. If no bonus is provided, the default value is used. This behavior simplifies function usage and ensures a consistent default value is applied.

Multiple Default Parameters

Functions can have multiple default parameters, allowing for more complex default behavior.

```typescript
// Function to generate a course description
function generateCourseDescription(
    courseName: string,
    instructor: string = "Anna",
    duration: number = 4
): string {
    return `${courseName} by ${instructor}, Duration: ${duration} weeks.`;
}


// Using the function with different combinations of parameters
const description1 = generateCourseDescription("TypeScript Basics");
const description2 = generateCourseDescription("Advanced TypeScript", "John", 6);


console.log(description1); // Output: TypeScript Basics by Anna, Duration: 4 weeks.
console.log(description2); // Output: Advanced TypeScript by John, Duration: 6 weeks.
```

Here, **generateCourseDescription** provides default values for **instructor** and **duration**. The function can be called with varying numbers of arguments, showcasing the flexibility of default parameters.

Rest Parameters and Variadic Functions

Rest parameters allow functions to accept an indefinite number of arguments as an array. This is particularly useful for creating variadic functions, which can operate on a variable number of inputs.

We will define a function that calculates the average score of students using rest parameters.

```
// Function to calculate the average score of students
function calculateAverageScore(...scores: number[]): number {
    const total = scores.reduce((sum, score) => sum + score, 0);
    return scores.length ? total / scores.length : 0;
}


// Using the function with different numbers of scores
const average1 = calculateAverageScore(85, 90, 78);
const average2 = calculateAverageScore(88, 76);


console.log(`Average Score 1: ${average1}`); // Output: Average Score 1: 84.33333333333333
console.log(`Average Score 2: ${average2}`); // Output: Average Score 2: 82
```

In the above code, **calculateAverageScore** uses rest parameters (**...scores**) to accept multiple score inputs. The function calculates the average of the provided scores, demonstrating how rest parameters enable functions to handle variable-length input arrays.

Creating Variadic Functions

Variadic functions use rest parameters to perform operations on a variable number of inputs. We will implement a function that calculates the total enrollment in multiple courses.

```
// Function to calculate total enrollment using rest parameters
function calculateTotalEnrollment(...enrollments: number[]): number {
    return enrollments.reduce((sum, enrollment) => sum + enrollment, 0);
}


// Using the function with different course enrollments
const totalEnrollment1 = calculateTotalEnrollment(30, 25, 40);
const totalEnrollment2 = calculateTotalEnrollment(20, 15, 35, 45);


console.log(`Total Enrollment 1: ${totalEnrollment1}`);
// Output: Total Enrollment 1: 95
console.log(`Total Enrollment 2: ${totalEnrollment2}`);
// Output: Total Enrollment 2: 115
```

In the above code, **calculateTotalEnrollment** is a variadic function that calculates the total number of students enrolled in multiple courses. The function uses rest parameters to accept multiple enrollment numbers, illustrating how variadic functions operate on flexible input sizes.

Combining Rest Parameters with Other Parameters

Rest parameters can be combined with other parameters, but they must be the last parameter in the function signature.

```
// Function to create a student report with additional comments
function createStudentReport(studentName: string, ...comments: string[]): string {
    return `Student: ${studentName}\nComments: ${comments.join(", ")}`;
}


// Using the function with different comments
const report1 = createStudentReport("Alice", "Excellent performance", "Needs improvement in math");
const report2 = createStudentReport("Bob", "Outstanding attendance");


console.log(report1);
console.log(report2);
```

In the above code, **createStudentReport** accepts a student name and an arbitrary number of comments as rest parameters. The function generates a report string, demonstrating how rest parameters work alongside other parameters.

Function Overloads

In TypeScript, function overloading allows you to define multiple function signatures for the same function name. This means you can create a single function that can handle different types and numbers of arguments, providing flexibility and readability when dealing with varying input scenarios.

What is an Overloaded Function?

An overloaded function is a function that has multiple type signatures but a single implementation. Each signature describes a different way to call the function, specifying the types and numbers of parameters and the return type. The implementation of the function decides what to do based on the provided arguments.

The primary purpose of function overloading is to enable a function to perform different tasks based on the arguments passed to it. By defining multiple signatures, you can ensure type safety while allowing the function to handle a variety of inputs.

Function overloads are particularly useful in scenarios where:

1. You need a function to handle various input types and perform different operations based on those types.
2. The function needs to support different numbers of parameters, each requiring different processing logic.
3. Depending on the input, the function may need to return different types of values.
4. Overloads improve code readability by providing clear and specific signatures for different use cases.
5. When working with external libraries or APIs that have overloaded functions, implementing similar overloads can ensure seamless integration.

Sample Program

We will implement a practical example in our project where function overloads are useful. Consider a scenario where we want to create a function that retrieves student information from different sources, such as a student ID or a student name. Depending on the input type (number or string), the function will return different information.

Defining Function Overloads

We will define overloads for a **getStudentInfo** function, specifying different signatures for different input types.

```
// Function overload signatures for getStudentInfo

function getStudentInfo(id: number): { id: number; name: string; score: number };
```

```typescript
function getStudentInfo(name: string): { id: number; name: string; score: number }[];


// Implementing the function
function getStudentInfo(param: number | string): { id: number; name: string; score: number } | { id: number; name: string; score: number }[] {
    // Mock student data
    const students = [
        { id: 1, name: "Alice", score: 85 },
        { id: 2, name: "Bob", score: 90 },
        { id: 3, name: "Charlie", score: 78 }
    ];

    // Check the type of the parameter and return appropriate data
    if (typeof param === "number") {
        return students.find(student => student.id === param) || { id: 0, name: "Not Found", score: 0 };
    } else {
        return students.filter(student => student.name.toLowerCase().includes(param.toLowerCase()));
    }
}
```

}

In the above code, the **getStudentInfo** function has two overload signatures:

- One that takes a **number** as an argument and returns a single student object.
- Another that takes a **string** as an argument and returns an array of student objects that match the name.

Using the Overloaded Function

We can call the **getStudentInfo** function with either an ID or a name to retrieve the corresponding student information.

```
// Retrieving student information by ID
const studentById = getStudentInfo(1);
console.log("Student by ID:", studentById);


// Retrieving student information by name
const studentsByName = getStudentInfo("b");
console.log("Students by Name:", studentsByName);
```

Here, the function is called twice: once with a student ID (**1**) and once with a name (**"b"**). The output will show different results based on the input type.

Function Overloads with Multiple Parameters

We will extend the example by adding another overload that allows retrieving students based on a combination of ID and minimum score.

```
// Additional overload signature for getStudentInfo
function getStudentInfo(id: number, minScore: number): { id: number; name: string; score: number };
```

```typescript
// Extending the implementation
function getStudentInfo(param: number | string, minScore?: number): { id: number; name: string; score: number } | { id: number; name: string; score: number }[] {
    // Mock student data
    const students = [
        { id: 1, name: "Alice", score: 85 },
        { id: 2, name: "Bob", score: 90 },
        { id: 3, name: "Charlie", score: 78 }
    ];


    // Check if minScore is provided for the ID overload
    if (typeof param === "number" && minScore !== undefined) {
        return students.find(student => student.id === param && student.score >= minScore) || { id: 0, name: "Not Found", score: 0 };
    }


    // Check the type of the parameter and return appropriate data
    if (typeof param === "number") {
        return students.find(student => student.id ===
```

```
param) || { id: 0, name: "Not Found", score: 0 };
    } else {
        return students.filter(student => student.name.toLowerCase().includes(param.toLowerCase()));
    }
}


// Using the additional overload
const studentByIdAndScore = getStudentInfo(1, 80);
console.log("Student by ID and Score:", studentByIdAndScore);
```

In this extended example, we added another overload signature that takes both an ID and a minimum score as arguments. The implementation checks if the minimum score is provided and returns the student only if the conditions are met.

Arrow, Callback and Higher-Order Functions

Arrow Functions

Arrow functions are a more concise way to write functions in JavaScript and TypeScript. They use a simplified syntax that makes the code easier to read and understand. Arrow functions also have a unique feature: they don't have their own **this** context. Instead, they inherit **this** from the surrounding code, which can be particularly useful in certain scenarios.

Syntax of Arrow Functions

Arrow functions use the **=>** syntax and can omit the **function** keyword. Given below is the basic syntax:

```
// Arrow function syntax
```

```
const add = (a: number, b: number): number => {
    return a + b;
};
```

The above code snippet defines an arrow function **add** that takes two parameters **a** and **b** and returns their sum. The parentheses around the parameters are optional if there is only one parameter.

Using Arrow Functions

We will use arrow functions to simplify some operations in our project.

```
// Array of student scores
const studentScores = [85, 90, 78, 92, 88];


// Using arrow function to calculate the average score
const calculateAverage = (scores: number[]): number => {
    const total = scores.reduce((sum, score) => sum + score, 0);
    return scores.length ? total / scores.length : 0;
};


// Calculating average score using the arrow function
const averageScore = calculateAverage(studentScores);
console.log(`Average Score: ${averageScore}`); // Output: Average Score: 86.6
```

In the above code, we use an arrow function **calculateAverage** to compute the average score of students. The arrow function provides a concise way to express the calculation logic.

Arrow Functions vs. Regular Functions

Arrow functions differ from regular functions in several ways, particularly in how they handle the **this** context.

```
// Regular function with its own this context
const instructor = {
    name: "Anna",
    courses: ["TypeScript Basics", "Advanced TypeScript"],
    listCourses: function () {
        this.courses.forEach(function (course) {
            console.log(`${this.name} teaches ${course}`); // this.name is undefined
        });
    }
};


// Calling the method
instructor.listCourses(); // Error: Cannot read property 'name' of undefined


// Fixing the error with an arrow function
const instructorFixed = {
    name: "Anna",
```

```
    courses: ["TypeScript Basics", "Advanced
TypeScript"],

    listCourses: function () {

        this.courses.forEach((course) => {

            console.log(`${this.name} teaches
${course}`); // this.name is "Anna"

        });

    }
};


// Calling the method

instructorFixed.listCourses(); // Output: Anna teaches
TypeScript Basics, Anna teaches Advanced TypeScript
```

In the first example, the regular function inside **forEach** creates its own **this** context, causing **this.name** to be **undefined**. By using an arrow function, which doesn't have its own **this**, we can correctly reference **this.name** from the outer function.

Callback Functions

Callback functions are functions passed as arguments to other functions. They allow code to be executed after a specific task is completed. Callbacks are often used in asynchronous programming and event handling.

Defining and Using Callback Functions

We will use callback functions to handle student enrollment in a course, where we want to execute a specific action after enrollment is complete.

```
// Function to enroll a student with a callback

function enrollStudent(student: string, callback:
```

```typescript
(message: string) => void): void {
    // Simulate enrollment process
    console.log(`Enrolling student: ${student}`);
    setTimeout(() => {
        // Enrollment complete, execute callback
        callback(`Student ${student} has been successfully enrolled.`);
    }, 2000); // Simulated delay
}


// Callback function to display a message
const displayMessage = (message: string): void => {
    console.log(message);
};


// Enrolling a student and using the callback
enrollStudent("Alice", displayMessage);
```

In the above code, the **enrollStudent** function takes a student name and a callback function as parameters. The callback function is executed after a simulated enrollment process, demonstrating how callbacks work in asynchronous operations.

Handling Multiple Callbacks

We can also pass multiple callback functions to handle different stages of a process.

```typescript
// Function to enroll a student with multiple callbacks
```

```
function enrollStudentWithCallbacks(
    student: string,
    onSuccess: (message: string) => void,
    onError: (error: string) => void
): void {
    // Simulate enrollment process
    console.log(`Enrolling student: ${student}`);
    setTimeout(() => {
        // Simulate a condition for success or error
        const isSuccess = Math.random() > 0.5;
        if (isSuccess) {
            onSuccess(`Student ${student} has been successfully enrolled.`);
        } else {
            onError(`Failed to enroll student ${student}. Please try again.`);
        }
    }, 2000); // Simulated delay
}

// Callback functions for success and error
const onSuccess = (message: string): void => {
```

```typescript
    console.log(message);
};

const onError = (error: string): void => {
    console.error(error);
};


// Enrolling a student with callbacks
enrollStudentWithCallbacks("Bob", onSuccess, onError);
```

In the above code, we define **enrollStudentWithCallbacks** with separate callbacks for success and error handling. The function randomly determines whether the enrollment is successful and calls the appropriate callback.

Higher-Order Functions

Higher-order functions are functions that can take other functions as arguments or return functions as their result. They are a key feature of functional programming and are commonly used for tasks like event handling, composition, and iteration.

Using Higher-Order Functions

We will create a higher-order function in our project to apply a discount to student scores based on a condition.

```typescript
// Higher-order function to apply a discount
function applyDiscount(
    scores: number[],
    discountFunction: (score: number) => number
): number[] {
```

```
    return scores.map(discountFunction);
}


// Discount function to reduce score by 10%
const discount10Percent = (score: number): number => score * 0.9;


// Using the higher-order function to apply the discount
const originalScores = [85, 90, 78, 92];
const discountedScores = applyDiscount(originalScores, discount10Percent);


console.log("Original Scores:", originalScores);
console.log("Discounted Scores:", discountedScores);
```

In the above code, **applyDiscount** is a higher-order function that takes an array of scores and a **discountFunction** as arguments. The **discountFunction** is applied to each score using the **map** method, demonstrating how higher-order functions can operate on data using other functions.

Returning Functions from Higher-Order Functions

Higher-order functions can also return functions, enabling more dynamic behavior.

```
// Higher-order function to create a multiplier
function createMultiplier(multiplier: number): (value: number) => number {
    return (value: number) => value * multiplier;
```

```
}

// Creating multiplier functions
const double = createMultiplier(2);
const triple = createMultiplier(3);

// Using the multiplier functions
console.log("Double of 5:", double(5)); // Output: Double of 5: 10
console.log("Triple of 5:", triple(5)); // Output: Triple of 5: 15
```

In the above code, **createMultiplier** is a higher-order function that returns a function to multiply a value by a specified multiplier. The returned functions, **double** and **triple**, demonstrate how higher-order functions can create reusable logic.

Summary

To quickly summarize, we started with function types and signatures, learning how to define and use different function declarations, including regular functions, function expressions, and arrow functions. Function signatures were highlighted as a way to ensure type safety by specifying parameters and return types. We then delved into optional and default parameters, which allow functions to handle varying input scenarios. Optional parameters enable arguments to be omitted, while default parameters provide fallback values when no argument is supplied. Rest parameters were introduced to support variadic functions, which can accept a variable number of arguments, enhancing the adaptability of functions.

Function overloading was also explored into detail, demonstrating how a single function can have multiple signatures, each handling different types and numbers of arguments. This feature was applied in our project, allowing the **getStudentInfo** function to retrieve student data based on different criteria. The chapter also covered arrow functions, emphasizing their concise syntax and unique handling of **this** context. We contrasted arrow functions with regular functions, illustrating how arrow functions can simplify code and maintain the desired context in callbacks.

Lastly, we explored callback and higher-order functions. Callbacks were used for asynchronous operations, enabling functions to be passed as arguments and executed upon task completion. Higher-order functions were demonstrated as functions that take or return other functions, showcasing their utility in creating flexible and reusable code. These concepts provided a comprehensive understanding of TypeScript functions, equipping us with the skills to write robust and efficient code in our ongoing project.

Chapter 4: Complex Types and Union Types

Chapter Overview

We will look at union types and complex types in this chapter, which enable more accurate and flexible data modeling. We will start by looking at union and intersection types, which allow you to define variables with multiple types or combine multiple types into one. These ideas are critical for developing adaptable and robust code that can handle a variety of data structures in our "Anna's TS Coaching" project.

Next, we will look at type guards and type assertions, which improve type safety by allowing you to narrow down types at runtime and explicitly inform the TypeScript compiler about a variable's expected type. These techniques will help you write more dependable and error-free code, especially when dealing with complex data structures. We will also look at literal types and type aliases, which allow you to define specific values and reusable custom types in your code, making it more expressive and maintainable.

We will also go over nullable types and optional properties, which will show you how to deal with values that are missing or undefined. Understanding how to work with nullable types and optional properties ensures that your code can handle missing data without throwing runtime errors. Finally, we will look at advanced object types like mapped types and conditional types, which allow you to perform sophisticated type transformations and model complex data relationships. This chapter will provide you with a better understanding of TypeScript's type system and its ability to manage complex data types effectively.

Union and Intersection Types

In TypeScript, union and intersection types allow you to create more flexible and powerful type definitions. They enable you to define variables and structures that can hold different kinds of data, making your code adaptable to various scenarios. We will explore these types in detail and see how they can be applied in our project.

Union Types

Union types allow a variable to hold more than one type. They are defined using the pipe (|) symbol, which represents a logical "or." A union type is useful when a value can be one of several types, providing flexibility while maintaining type safety.

Defining Union Types

Suppose we want to store either a string or a number in a variable to represent a student's ID, which could be a numeric ID or a custom alphanumeric code.

```
// Defining a union type for student ID
```

```typescript
type StudentID = number | string;

// Example usage of union type
let studentId1: StudentID = 12345; // Numeric ID
let studentId2: StudentID = "A1234"; // Alphanumeric ID

console.log(`Student ID 1: ${studentId1}`);
console.log(`Student ID 2: ${studentId2}`);
```

In the above code, **StudentID** is a union type that can hold either a **number** or a **string**. The variables **studentId1** and **studentId2** demonstrate how union types enable the use of multiple types for a single variable.

Union Types

We will use union types in a function that calculates tuition fees for a student, depending on whether the student has a discount code (string) or a fixed discount amount (number).

```typescript
// Function to calculate tuition fee with union type
function calculateTuitionFee(baseFee: number, discount: number | string): number {
    if (typeof discount === "number") {
        // Subtract the discount amount from the base fee
        return baseFee - discount;
    } else if (typeof discount === "string") {
        // Check for specific discount codes
        if (discount === "HALFPRICE") {
```

```
        return baseFee / 2; // 50% discount

    } else if (discount === "FREESHIP") {

        return baseFee - 20; // $20 off for shipping

    }

}

return baseFee; // No discount applied

}
```

```
// Using the function with different discounts

const baseFee = 100;

const feeWithAmountDiscount = calculateTuitionFee(baseFee, 15); // Using number

const feeWithCodeDiscount = calculateTuitionFee(baseFee, "HALFPRICE"); // Using string


console.log(`Fee with Amount Discount: $${feeWithAmountDiscount}`); // Output: Fee with Amount Discount: $85

console.log(`Fee with Code Discount: $${feeWithCodeDiscount}`);    // Output: Fee with Code Discount: $50
```

In this function, **calculateTuitionFee** uses a union type for the **discount** parameter, allowing it to handle both numeric and string discounts. The function checks the type of **discount** at runtime and applies the appropriate logic.

Intersection Types

Intersection types allow you to combine multiple types into a single type. They are defined using the ampersand (**&**) symbol, representing a logical "and." An intersection type requires that a variable satisfy all the combined types, making it useful for merging interfaces or type definitions.

Defining Intersection Types

We will define an intersection type to represent a student who is both enrolled in a course and has a profile.

```
// Defining interfaces for enrollment and profile
interface Enrollment {
    courseId: number;
    status: string;
}


interface Profile {
    name: string;
    age: number;
}


// Intersection type combining enrollment and profile
type EnrolledStudent = Enrollment & Profile;


// Example usage of intersection type
const student: EnrolledStudent = {
```

```
    courseId: 101,
    status: "active",
    name: "Alice",
    age: 20
};
```

```
console.log(`Student Name: ${student.name}`);
console.log(`Course ID: ${student.courseId}`);
console.log(`Enrollment Status: ${student.status}`);
```

In the above code, **EnrolledStudent** is an intersection type combining the **Enrollment** and **Profile** interfaces. The **student** variable must satisfy both interfaces, ensuring that it contains all the necessary properties.

Intersection Types

We will use intersection types in a function that updates both the enrollment and profile information of a student.

```
// Function to update student information using intersection type
function updateStudentInfo(student: EnrolledStudent, newInfo: Partial<EnrolledStudent>): EnrolledStudent {
    return { ...student, ...newInfo };
}


// Updating student information
const updatedStudent = updateStudentInfo(student, {
```

```
status: "inactive", age: 21 });
```

```
console.log(`Updated Student Status:
${updatedStudent.status}`);
```

```
console.log(`Updated Student Age:
${updatedStudent.age}`);
```

In this function, **updateStudentInfo** uses the **EnrolledStudent** intersection type to update a student's information. The function accepts an **EnrolledStudent** object and a **Partial<EnrolledStudent>** object, allowing selective updates to the student's information while maintaining type safety.

Sample Program

Suppose we want to manage course information, including both online and in-person courses. Online courses have a URL, while in-person courses have a location. We will use union and intersection types to represent this data structure.

```
// Defining interfaces for online and in-person courses
interface OnlineCourse {
    title: string;
    url: string;
}


interface InPersonCourse {
    title: string;
    location: string;
}
```

```typescript
// Union type for course
type Course = OnlineCourse | InPersonCourse;


// Function to display course details
function displayCourseDetails(course: Course): void {
    console.log(`Course Title: ${course.title}`);
    if ("url" in course) {
        console.log(`Course URL: ${course.url}`);
    } else if ("location" in course) {
        console.log(`Course Location: ${course.location}`);
    }
}


// Using the function with different course types
const onlineCourse: Course = { title: "TypeScript Basics", url: "https://example.com/ts-basics" };
const inPersonCourse: Course = { title: "Advanced TypeScript", location: "Room 101" };

displayCourseDetails(onlineCourse); // Output: Course Title: TypeScript Basics, Course URL: https://example.com/ts-basics
```

```
displayCourseDetails(inPersonCourse); // Output: Course 
Title: Advanced TypeScript, Course Location: Room 101
```

In the above code, the **Course** type is a union of **OnlineCourse** and **InPersonCourse**, allowing us to represent courses that can be either online or in-person. The **displayCourseDetails** function uses type narrowing to determine the type of course and display the appropriate details.

Type Guards and Type Assertions

Type Guards

Type guards are techniques used to determine the specific type of a variable at runtime. They help ensure that operations are performed on the correct type, improving type safety and preventing runtime errors. Type guards are particularly useful when working with union types, as they allow you to narrow down the type of a variable and access its properties safely.

Type guards are usually implemented using conditional checks, such as **typeof**, **instanceof**, or custom type predicates.

'typeof' for Type Guards

The typeof operator checks the type of a variable, making it useful for distinguishing between primitive types like string, number, and boolean.

```
// Function to handle different input types using typeof
function processInput(input: number | string) {
    if (typeof input === "number") {
        console.log(`The number is ${input.toFixed(2)}`);
    } else if (typeof input === "string") {
        console.log(`The string length is ${input.length}`);
    }
}
```

```
// Using the function with different types
processInput(42); // Output: The number is 42.00
processInput("Hello"); // Output: The string length is 5
```

In the above code, **processInput** uses **typeof** to check the type of **input** and perform operations specific to each type.

'instanceof' for Type Guards

The instanceof operator checks if an object is an instance of a particular class, making it useful for distinguishing between class instances.

```
// Classes for OnlineCourse and InPersonCourse
class OnlineCourse {
    constructor(public title: string, public url: string) {}
}


class InPersonCourse {
    constructor(public title: string, public location: string) {}
}


// Function to display course details using instanceof
function displayCourse(course: OnlineCourse | InPersonCourse) {
    console.log(`Course Title: ${course.title}`);
```

```
    if (course instanceof OnlineCourse) {
        console.log(`Course URL: ${course.url}`);
    } else if (course instanceof InPersonCourse) {
        console.log(`Course Location: ${course.location}`);
    }
}
```

```
// Using the function with different course types
const onlineCourse = new OnlineCourse("TypeScript Basics", "https://example.com/ts-basics");

const inPersonCourse = new InPersonCourse("Advanced TypeScript", "Room 101");


displayCourse(onlineCourse); // Output: Course Title: TypeScript Basics, Course URL: https://example.com/ts-basics

displayCourse(inPersonCourse); // Output: Course Title: Advanced TypeScript, Course Location: Room 101
```

In the above code, **displayCourse** uses **instanceof** to determine the type of course and display the appropriate details.

Custom Type Predicates

Custom type predicates allow you to define more complex type guards by creating functions that return a boolean and use the is keyword to narrow the type.

```
// Interface for a course with a URL
```

```typescript
interface HasUrl {
    url: string;
}


// Type predicate to check if an object has a URL
function hasUrl(course: any): course is HasUrl {
    return (course as HasUrl).url !== undefined;
}


// Function to display course details using a custom type guard
function displayCourseDetails(course: OnlineCourse | InPersonCourse) {
    console.log(`Course Title: ${course.title}`);
    if (hasUrl(course)) {
        console.log(`Course URL: ${course.url}`);
    } else {
        console.log(`Course Location: ${course.location}`);
    }
}
```

```
// Using the function with different course types
displayCourseDetails(onlineCourse);
displayCourseDetails(inPersonCourse);
```

In the above code, **hasUrl** is a custom type predicate that checks if an object has a **url** property. The **displayCourseDetails** function uses this predicate to determine the course type.

Type Assertions

Type assertions are a way to explicitly tell the TypeScript compiler about the type of a variable, allowing you to override the inferred type. They are useful when you know more about the type of a variable than the compiler does, but should be used cautiously to avoid runtime errors.

Type assertions are helpful when:

- You need to narrow a type when the compiler cannot.
- You're working with data from external sources where the type is known but not easily inferred.
- You need to access properties of a variable that are known but not recognized by the compiler.

Type assertions do not perform any runtime checks; they only affect the compile-time type checking.

Type Assertions Syntax

Type assertions can be written in two ways:

- Using the **as** keyword:

```
let someValue: any = "This is a string";
let strLength: number = (someValue as string).length;
console.log(strLength); // Output: 16
```

Using angle bracket syntax (not recommended in JSX):

```
let someValue: any = "This is a string";
let strLength: number = (<string>someValue).length;
```

```
console.log(strLength); // Output: 16
```

In both examples, **someValue** is asserted as a **string**, allowing access to string-specific properties and methods.

Type Assertion Implementation

We will implement type assertions in a situation, where we have data coming from an external API and need to assert the types.

```
// Example data from an API
const apiData: any = {
    id: 1,
    name: "Alice",
    courses: ["TypeScript Basics", "Advanced TypeScript"]
};


// Defining an interface for the expected data structure
interface StudentData {
    id: number;
    name: string;
    courses: string[];
}


// Using type assertion to assert the type of apiData
const studentData = apiData as StudentData;
```

```
// Accessing properties of the asserted type
console.log(`Student ID: ${studentData.id}`);
console.log(`Student Name: ${studentData.name}`);
console.log(`Courses: ${studentData.courses.join(", ")}`);
```

In the above code, we assert **apiData** as **StudentData** using the **as** keyword, allowing us to safely access the properties of the data structure.

Type Assertions for DOM Manipulation

Type assertions are also commonly used when working with the DOM to access element-specific properties.

```
// Accessing an HTML element and asserting its type
const inputElement = document.getElementById("myInput") as HTMLInputElement;


// Accessing the value property of the input element
inputElement.value = "Hello, TypeScript!";


console.log(inputElement.value); // Output: Hello, TypeScript!
```

In the above code, we use a type assertion to specify that **inputElement** is an **HTMLInputElement**, allowing access to the **value** property.

Literal Types and Type Aliases

In TypeScript, literal types and type aliases allow you to create more precise and readable type definitions, improving code clarity and safety. Literal types restrict a variable to a specific value or set of values, while type aliases allow you to define custom types for complex structures. We will explore both concepts and apply them in our project.

Literal Types

Literal types are specific types that represent exact values, rather than just types like **string** or **number**. They can be string, number, or boolean literals. By using literal types, you can restrict variables to specific values, enhancing type safety and enabling the compiler to catch errors at compile time.

Defining Literal Types

Suppose we want to define specific statuses for student enrollment: "active," "inactive," or "graduated." We can use string literal types to achieve this.

```
// Defining string literal types for student status

type StudentStatus = "active" | "inactive" | "graduated";


// Using literal types in a function

function getStudentStatus(status: StudentStatus): string {

    switch (status) {

        case "active":

            return "The student is currently enrolled.";

        case "inactive":

            return "The student is not enrolled at the moment.";

        case "graduated":
```

```
            return "The student has graduated.";
        default:
            return "Unknown status.";
    }
}
```

```
// Example usage of the function with literal types
console.log(getStudentStatus("active")); // Output: The student is currently enrolled.
console.log(getStudentStatus("graduated")); // Output: The student has graduated.
```

In the above code, **StudentStatus** is a string literal type that restricts the **status** parameter to specific values. The **getStudentStatus** function can only accept these defined values, ensuring type safety.

Literal Types in Conditional Logic

Literal types can also be used to represent numeric values or specific conditions.

```
// Defining numeric literal types for grading
type Grade = 1 | 2 | 3 | 4 | 5;


// Function to get feedback based on grade
function getFeedback(grade: Grade): string {
    switch (grade) {
        case 1:
```

```
        return "Excellent work!";
    case 2:
        return "Great job!";
    case 3:
        return "Good effort.";
    case 4:
        return "Needs improvement.";
    case 5:
        return "Unsatisfactory.";
    default:
        return "Invalid grade.";
    }
}


// Example usage of the function with numeric literal types
console.log(getFeedback(1)); // Output: Excellent work!
console.log(getFeedback(3)); // Output: Good effort.
```

In the above code, **Grade** is a numeric literal type representing possible grade values. The **getFeedback** function provides feedback based on the specific grade, ensuring that only valid grades are processed.

Type Aliases

Type aliases allow you to create custom type definitions, providing a more readable and maintainable way to define complex types. Type aliases are especially useful when you have repetitive type definitions or need to represent intricate data structures.

Creating Type Aliases

We will define type aliases for student and course structures in our project to simplify type definitions.

```
// Defining a type alias for student
type Student = {
    id: number;
    name: string;
    status: StudentStatus;
    courses: string[];
};


// Defining a type alias for course
type Course = {
    id: number;
    title: string;
    duration: number; // Duration in weeks
};


// Function to enroll a student in a course
function enrollStudentInCourse(student: Student, course: Course): void {
```

```typescript
    console.log(`Enrolling ${student.name} in the course: ${course.title}`);
    student.courses.push(course.title);
}


// Example usage of type aliases
const student1: Student = {
    id: 1,
    name: "Alice",
    status: "active",
    courses: []
};

const course1: Course = {
    id: 101,
    title: "TypeScript Basics",
    duration: 4
};

enrollStudentInCourse(student1, course1);
console.log(`${student1.name} is enrolled in: ${student1.courses.join(", ")}`); // Output: Alice is
```

enrolled in: TypeScript Basics

In the above code, **Student** and **Course** are type aliases representing the structure of a student and a course. The **enrollStudentInCourse** function uses these aliases to ensure that the correct data structure is passed as arguments, making the code more readable and maintainable.

Type Aliases for Unions and Intersections

Type aliases can also be used to define unions and intersections, simplifying complex type definitions.

```typescript
// Defining a union type alias for payment methods
type PaymentMethod = "credit" | "debit" | "paypal";


// Defining an intersection type alias for a course with payment options
type PaidCourse = Course & {
    price: number;
    paymentMethod: PaymentMethod;
};


// Function to purchase a course
function purchaseCourse(student: Student, course: PaidCourse): void {
    console.log(`${student.name} is purchasing the course: ${course.title} for $${course.price} using ${course.paymentMethod}`);
}
```

```typescript
// Example usage of type aliases with unions and intersections

const paidCourse: PaidCourse = {

    id: 102,

    title: "Advanced TypeScript",

    duration: 6,

    price: 100,

    paymentMethod: "credit"

};


purchaseCourse(student1, paidCourse);
```

In the above code, **PaymentMethod** is a union type alias representing accepted payment methods, and **PaidCourse** is an intersection type alias combining **Course** and additional properties. The **purchaseCourse** function uses these aliases to handle course purchases, demonstrating how type aliases can simplify complex types.

Sample Program

Suppose we want to manage course enrollment and provide feedback based on student performance. We will use literal types and type aliases to structure the data and operations.

```typescript
// Defining literal types for feedback levels

type FeedbackLevel = "excellent" | "good" | "average" | "poor";


// Defining a type alias for feedback
```

```typescript
type Feedback = {
    studentId: number;
    courseId: number;
    level: FeedbackLevel;
    comments: string;
};


// Function to give feedback
function giveFeedback(feedback: Feedback): void {
    console.log(`Feedback for Student ID: ${feedback.studentId}, Course ID: ${feedback.courseId}`);
    console.log(`Level: ${feedback.level}`);
    console.log(`Comments: ${feedback.comments}`);
}


// Example usage of feedback with literal types and type aliases
const feedback1: Feedback = {
    studentId: 1,
    courseId: 101,
    level: "excellent",
    comments: "Outstanding performance in all assignments
```

```
and exams."
};


giveFeedback(feedback1);
```

In the above code, **FeedbackLevel** is a string literal type representing feedback levels, and **Feedback** is a type alias for feedback data. The **giveFeedback** function uses these definitions to handle feedback, illustrating how literal types and type aliases improve type safety and code organization.

Nullable Types and Optional Properties

In TypeScript, nullable types and optional properties allow you to work with data that may be absent or undefined. This feature is particularly useful when dealing with dynamic data structures or incomplete data. In this, we will explore how to define and use nullable types and optional properties, and how optional chaining can make accessing nested properties safer and more concise. We will apply these concepts to our project.

Nullable Types

Nullable types are types that can be either a specific type or **null** or **undefined**. They are useful when a variable or property might not have a value initially or under certain conditions.

Defining Nullable Types

In TypeScript, you can define nullable types by using the union type syntax with **null** and **undefined**.

```
// Defining nullable types for student feedback
type NullableFeedback = string | null | undefined;


// Function to provide feedback with nullable types
function provideFeedback(feedback: NullableFeedback): string {
```

```
    if (feedback === null) {
        return "No feedback provided.";
    } else if (feedback === undefined) {
        return "Feedback is pending.";
    } else {
        return `Feedback: ${feedback}`;
    }
}


// Example usage of nullable types
console.log(provideFeedback("Great job!")); // Output: Feedback: Great job!
console.log(provideFeedback(null)); // Output: No feedback provided.
console.log(provideFeedback(undefined)); // Output: Feedback is pending.
```

In the above code, **NullableFeedback** is a type alias that allows a **string**, **null**, or **undefined**. The **provideFeedback** function handles each case appropriately, demonstrating how nullable types can manage missing or pending data.

Applying Nullable Types

Now, let's apply nullable types in our project by allowing a student's feedback and enrollment status to be nullable.

```
// Updated Student type with nullable feedback and status
type Student = {
```

```typescript
    id: number;
    name: string;
    status: StudentStatus | null; // Nullable status
    courses: string[];
    feedback: NullableFeedback; // Nullable feedback
};


// Function to update student status
function updateStudentStatus(student: Student, newStatus: StudentStatus | null): void {
    student.status = newStatus;
    console.log(`Student ${student.name}'s status updated to: ${newStatus ?? "Unknown"}`);
}


// Example usage
const student1: Student = {
    id: 1,
    name: "Alice",
    status: null, // Initially unknown
    courses: ["TypeScript Basics"],
    feedback: "Excellent progress!"
```

```
};
```

```
updateStudentStatus(student1, "active");

updateStudentStatus(student1, null); // Setting status to unknown
```

In the above code, the **Student** type now includes nullable properties for **status** and **feedback**. The **updateStudentStatus** function updates a student's status and handles **null** as an unknown status.

Optional Properties

Optional properties are properties that may or may not be present in an object. They are useful when working with data structures that might have missing or optional fields.

Defining Optional Properties

Optional properties are defined by adding a question mark (**?**) after the property name in the type definition.

```
// Defining a Course type with optional properties
type Course = {
    id: number;
    title: string;
    duration: number; // Duration in weeks
    description?: string; // Optional description
};


// Function to display course information
function displayCourseInfo(course: Course): void {
```

```
    console.log(`Course Title: ${course.title}`);
    console.log(`Duration: ${course.duration} weeks`);
    if (course.description) {
        console.log(`Description: ${course.description}`);
    } else {
        console.log("No description available.");
    }
}


// Example usage of optional properties
const course1: Course = {
    id: 101,
    title: "TypeScript Basics",
    duration: 4
};


const course2: Course = {
    id: 102,
    title: "Advanced TypeScript",
    duration: 6,
    description: "An in-depth look into TypeScript's
```

```
advanced features."
};
```

```
displayCourseInfo(course1); // Output: No description available.

displayCourseInfo(course2); // Output: Description: An in-depth look into TypeScript's advanced features.
```

In the above code, the **Course** type includes an optional **description** property. The **displayCourseInfo** function checks for the presence of the **description** property and handles it accordingly.

Using Optional Properties

We will use optional properties in our project by allowing some courses to have optional prerequisites.

```
// Updated Course type with optional prerequisites
type Course = {
    id: number;
    title: string;
    duration: number;
    prerequisites?: string[]; // Optional prerequisites
};


// Function to display course details with prerequisites
function displayCourseDetails(course: Course): void {
    console.log(`Course Title: ${course.title}`);
```

```
        console.log(`Duration: ${course.duration} weeks`);
        if (course.prerequisites) {
            console.log(`Prerequisites: ${course.prerequisites.join(", ")}`);
        } else {
            console.log("No prerequisites required.");
        }
    }


// Example usage with optional prerequisites
const course3: Course = {
    id: 103,
    title: "Mastering TypeScript",
    duration: 8,
    prerequisites: ["TypeScript Basics", "Advanced TypeScript"]
};


displayCourseDetails(course1); // Output: No prerequisites required.
displayCourseDetails(course3); // Output: Prerequisites: TypeScript Basics, Advanced TypeScript
```

In the above code, the **Course** type includes optional **prerequisites**. The

displayCourseDetails function checks if the **prerequisites** property is present and displays it if available.

Optional Chaining

Optional chaining is a feature that allows you to safely access nested properties of an object without having to check each level for **null** or **undefined**. It uses the **?.** operator to short-circuit and return **undefined** if a property is not present.

Using Optional Chaining

We will use optional chaining to safely access nested properties in our project.

```
// Function to get a student's first course title using optional chaining

function getFirstCourseTitle(student: Student): string {

    return student.courses?.[0] ?? "No courses enrolled.";

}



// Example usage with optional chaining

const student2: Student = {

    id: 2,

    name: "Bob",

    status: "active",

    courses: [], // No courses enrolled

    feedback: undefined

};
```

```
console.log(getFirstCourseTitle(student1)); // Output: TypeScript Basics

console.log(getFirstCourseTitle(student2)); // Output: No courses enrolled.
```

In the above code, **getFirstCourseTitle** uses optional chaining to access the first course title in a student's **courses** array. If the array is empty or **undefined**, it returns a default message.

Optional Chaining with Nested Objects

Optional chaining can also be used with nested objects to access deep properties safely.

```
// Nested type alias for Student with Address
type Address = {
    street: string;
    city: string;
    country: string;
};


type StudentWithAddress = Student & {
    address?: Address; // Optional address
};


// Function to get the student's city using optional chaining
function getStudentCity(student: StudentWithAddress): string {
```

```
    return student.address?.city ?? "City not available.";
}
```

```
// Example usage with nested optional chaining
const studentWithAddress: StudentWithAddress = {
    ...student1,
    address: { street: "123 Main St", city: "Springfield", country: "USA" }
};
```

```
console.log(getStudentCity(studentWithAddress)); // Output: Springfield
console.log(getStudentCity(student2)); // Output: City not available.
```

In the above code, **getStudentCity** uses optional chaining to access the **city** property of a student's **address** object. If the **address** or **city** is missing, it returns a default message.

Sample Program

We will apply nullable types, optional properties, and optional chaining in our project to manage course and student information more effectively.

```
// Updated Student type with nullable feedback and status
type Student = {
    id: number;
    name: string;
```

```typescript
    status: StudentStatus | null;
    courses: string[];
    feedback: NullableFeedback;
};


// Updated Course type with optional description and prerequisites
type Course = {
    id: number;
    title: string;
    duration: number;
    description?: string;
    prerequisites?: string[];
};


// Function to get detailed student information using optional chaining
function getStudentInfo(student: Student): void {
    console.log(`Student Name: ${student.name}`);
    console.log(`Status: ${student.status ?? "Unknown"}`);
    console.log(`Enrolled Courses: ${student.courses.join(", ")}`);
```

```typescript
    console.log(`Feedback: ${student.feedback ?? "No feedback"}`);
}


// Function to display complete course details
function displayFullCourseDetails(course: Course): void {
    console.log(`Course Title: ${course.title}`);
    console.log(`Duration: ${course.duration} weeks`);
    console.log(`Description: ${course.description ?? "No description available."}`);
    console.log(`Prerequisites: ${course.prerequisites?.join(", ") ?? "None"}`);
}


// Example usage of the functions
const student3: Student = {
    id: 3,
    name: "Charlie",
    status: "inactive",
    courses: ["Advanced TypeScript"],
    feedback: null
};
```

```
const course4: Course = {
    id: 104,
    title: "TypeScript Masterclass",
    duration: 12
};
```

```
getStudentInfo(student3); // Output includes no feedback
displayFullCourseDetails(course4); // Output includes no description and no prerequisites
```

In the above code, we use nullable types, optional properties, and optional chaining to handle course and student data that may be incomplete or missing. This approach ensures that the application can gracefully handle situations where data is not available without causing runtime errors.

Advanced Object Types

Here, we will explore advanced object types in TypeScript, focusing on index signatures and recursive types. These features allow you to define more dynamic and complex data structures, providing flexibility when working with objects whose properties may not be known in advance or whose structure may be nested.

Index Signatures

Index signatures allow you to define the shape of objects with dynamic properties. They are used when the properties of an object are not known beforehand, or when you want to enforce a specific type for all property values.

Defining Index Signatures

An index signature defines a type for the keys and values of an object. The syntax uses square brackets `[ ]`, with a type annotation for the key and value.

```typescript
// Defining an index signature for a collection of courses
type CourseCollection = {
    [key: string]: string; // Key is a string, and value is a string
};


// Example usage of index signature
const courses: CourseCollection = {
    "101": "TypeScript Basics",
    "102": "Advanced TypeScript",
    "103": "TypeScript Masterclass"
};


console.log(`Course 101: ${courses["101"]}`); // Output: Course 101: TypeScript Basics
console.log(`Course 102: ${courses["102"]}`); // Output: Course 102: Advanced TypeScript
```

In the above code, **CourseCollection** is an index signature that allows any string key with a string value. The **courses** object uses this signature to store course titles with numeric keys represented as strings.

Implementing Index Signatures

We will apply index signatures in our project to manage a collection of student scores.

```typescript
// Defining an index signature for student scores
```

```typescript
type StudentScores = {
    [studentId: number]: number; // Key is a number (student ID), and value is a number (score)
};


// Function to calculate the average score
function calculateAverageScore(scores: StudentScores): number {
    const total = Object.values(scores).reduce((sum, score) => sum + score, 0);
    return total / Object.keys(scores).length;
}


// Example usage with index signatures
const scores: StudentScores = {
    1: 85,
    2: 92,
    3: 78,
    4: 88
};

console.log(`Average Score: ${calculateAverageScore(scores)}`); // Output: Average
```

```
Score: 85.75
```

In the above code, **StudentScores** is an index signature where keys are student IDs and values are their scores. The **calculateAverageScore** function computes the average score using the index signature, allowing dynamic access to student scores.

Recursive Types

Recursive types are types that refer to themselves in their own definition. They are useful for representing data structures that have a recursive or nested nature, such as trees, linked lists, or nested objects.

Defining Recursive Types

Recursive types are defined by referencing the type within its definition. We will consider a recursive type for a nested category structure.

```
// Defining a recursive type for categories
type Category = {
    name: string;
    subcategories?: Category[]; // Recursive reference to Category
};


// Example usage of recursive types
const categoryTree: Category = {
    name: "Programming",
    subcategories: [
        {
            name: "Web Development",
```

```
        subcategories: [
            { name: "Frontend" },
            { name: "Backend" }
        ]
    },
    { name: "Data Science" }
    ]
};


console.log(categoryTree);
```

In the above code, **Category** is a recursive type with a **name** and optional **subcategories**, which is an array of **Category** objects. The **categoryTree** demonstrates a nested category structure using the recursive type.

Implementing Recursive Types

We will use recursive types in our project to represent a curriculum with nested modules.

```
// Defining a recursive type for a curriculum module
type Module = {
    title: string;
    duration: number; // Duration in hours
    submodules?: Module[]; // Recursive reference to Module
};
```

```typescript
// Function to calculate the total duration of a curriculum
function calculateTotalDuration(module: Module): number {
    let total = module.duration;
    if (module.submodules) {
        for (const submodule of module.submodules) {
            total += calculateTotalDuration(submodule);
        }
    }
    return total;
}

// Example usage of recursive types in a curriculum
const curriculum: Module = {
    title: "TypeScript Mastery",
    duration: 5,
    submodules: [
        {
            title: "Basics",
            duration: 3,
            submodules: [
                { title: "Introduction", duration: 1 },
```

```
            { title: "Types", duration: 2 }
        ]
    },
    {
        title: "Advanced Concepts",
        duration: 4,
        submodules: [
            { title: "Generics", duration: 2 },
            { title: "Decorators", duration: 2 }
        ]
    }
  ]
};

console.log(`Total Curriculum Duration: ${calculateTotalDuration(curriculum)} hours`); // Output: Total Curriculum Duration: 17 hours
```

In the above code, **Module** is a recursive type representing a curriculum module with a **title**, **duration**, and optional **submodules**. The `calculateTotalDuration` function computes the total duration of a curriculum by recursively traversing the module structure.

Sample Program

We will integrate index signatures and recursive types into our project to manage dynamic student data and course structures.

```typescript
// Index signature for dynamic student records
type StudentRecord = {
    [studentId: number]: {
        name: string;
        score: number;
    };
};


// Function to display student records
function displayStudentRecords(records: StudentRecord): void {
    for (const id in records) {
        const student = records[id];
        console.log(`Student ID: ${id}, Name: ${student.name}, Score: ${student.score}`);
    }
}


// Example usage of index signatures for student records
const studentRecords: StudentRecord = {
    1: { name: "Alice", score: 85 },
    2: { name: "Bob", score: 92 },
```

```
        3: { name: "Charlie", score: 78 }
};

displayStudentRecords(studentRecords);


// Recursive type for course content
type CourseContent = {
    title: string;
    lessons: number;
    subcontent?: CourseContent[]; // Recursive reference to CourseContent
};


// Function to count total lessons in a course
function countTotalLessons(content: CourseContent): number {
    let total = content.lessons;
    if (content.subcontent) {
        for (const sub of content.subcontent) {
            total += countTotalLessons(sub);
        }
    }
```

```
    return total;
}


// Example usage of recursive types for course content
const courseContent: CourseContent = {
    title: "TypeScript Advanced Course",
    lessons: 5,
    subcontent: [
        {
            title: "Generics",
            lessons: 3,
            subcontent: [
                { title: "Introduction to Generics", lessons: 1 },
                { title: "Generic Functions", lessons: 2 }
            ]
        },
        {
            title: "Modules",
            lessons: 4
        }
```

```
        ]
};
```

```
console.log(`Total Lessons in Course:
${countTotalLessons(courseContent)}`); // Output: Total
Lessons in Course: 12
```

In this project application, index signatures and recursive types are used to manage dynamic student records and nested course content, providing a flexible and robust way to handle complex data structures.

Summary

Overall, this chapter looked at complex types and their applications, with a focus on improving code flexibility and robustness. We started by looking at union and intersection types, which allowed variables to hold multiple types or combine them into one. This allowed for greater adaptability in dealing with different data structures as well as more precise type definitions. In our project, we used these concepts to manage student and course data.

Next, we looked at type guards and type assertions, which provided tools for ensuring type safety during runtime. Type guards allowed us to refine types through runtime checks, whereas type assertions allowed us to explicitly specify a variable's type, improving type accuracy in situations where the compiler may not infer the correct type. These techniques were essential in dealing with dynamic and complex data structures. We then looked at literal types and type aliases, which improve type safety and code clarity by specifying specific values and reusable custom types. Literal types limited variables to exact values, whereas type aliases allowed for the concise definition of complex types. These features were implemented in our project to improve course and student data management.

We also looked at nullable types and optional properties, which helped us deal with missing or incomplete data gracefully. Nullable types allowed variables to be null or undefined, while optional properties allowed the definition of fields that were not always present in objects. We used these concepts to effectively manage course and student data while ensuring robust error handling. Finally, we explored the advanced object types like index signatures and recursive types. Index signatures made it easier to work with objects that had dynamic properties, whereas recursive types represented nested data structures. These advanced types provided greater flexibility in managing complex data, strengthening our project in its entirety.

Chapter 5: Classes and Interfaces

Chapter Overview

Classes and interfaces are TypeScript's major object-oriented features, which will be covered in detail in this chapter. This chapter will help you understand how to structure and organize code efficiently, making it more modular and reusable. We begin by learning how to define and use classes, which are the fundamental building blocks for creating objects. Classes enable us to encapsulate data and functionality, thereby providing a blueprint for creating objects with specific properties and functions. Next, we will look at class inheritance and modifiers, which allow us to reuse code and create hierarchical class structures. Inheritance allows one class to inherit the properties and methods of another, making it easier to extend and modify existing classes. We will also go over access modifiers like public, private, and protected, which control the visibility and accessibility of class members while ensuring encapsulation and security.

We will then learn interfaces, which define contracts for classes by specifying the properties and methods that a class must implement. Interfaces ensure consistency across implementations, allowing for flexible and interchangeable code. And finally, we will also learn how to extend interfaces to create more complex type definitions, which will allow us to combine multiple interfaces into a single cohesive structure.

Working with Classes

Classes are a fundamental part of object-oriented programming in TypeScript. They provide a blueprint for creating objects with specific properties and methods, allowing you to encapsulate and organize your code effectively. In this section, we will learn to create classes, define class constructors and methods, and use access modifiers like **public**, **private**, and **protected** to control visibility and accessibility.

Creating Classes

In TypeScript, classes are defined using the **class** keyword. A class can have properties and methods, which define the behavior of the objects created from the class.

We will create a simple class in our project to represent a course.

```
// Defining a Course class
class Course {
    title: string;
    duration: number; // Duration in weeks
```

```
    // Method to display course details
    displayCourseInfo() {
        console.log(`Course Title: ${this.title}`);
        console.log(`Duration: ${this.duration} weeks`);
    }
}


// Creating an instance of the Course class
const course1 = new Course();
course1.title = "TypeScript Basics";
course1.duration = 4;


// Displaying course information
course1.displayCourseInfo();
// Output:
// Course Title: TypeScript Basics
// Duration: 4 weeks
```

In the above code, we define a **Course** class with two properties: **title** and **duration**. The **displayCourseInfo** method prints the course details. We then create an instance of the **Course** class and set its properties before calling the method.

Defining Class Constructors and Methods

A constructor is a special method used to initialize objects created from a class. It allows you to set initial values for properties when an object is instantiated.

Using Constructors

We will add a constructor to the **Course** class to initialize its properties.

```
// Defining a Course class with a constructor
class Course {
    title: string;
    duration: number; // Duration in weeks


    // Constructor to initialize properties
    constructor(title: string, duration: number) {
        this.title = title;
        this.duration = duration;
    }


    // Method to display course details
    displayCourseInfo() {
        console.log(`Course Title: ${this.title}`);
        console.log(`Duration: ${this.duration} weeks`);
    }
}
```

```typescript
// Creating an instance of the Course class using the constructor
const course2 = new Course("Advanced TypeScript", 6);

// Displaying course information
course2.displayCourseInfo();
// Output:
// Course Title: Advanced TypeScript
// Duration: 6 weeks
```

In the above code, the **Course** class includes a constructor that accepts **title** and **duration** as parameters, initializing the corresponding properties. This approach simplifies the creation of new course instances.

Defining Methods

Methods are functions defined within a class that operate on the object's properties. They encapsulate the behavior associated with the class.

We will add more methods to the **Course** class to handle course enrollment.

```typescript
// Enhancing the Course class with enrollment methods
class Course {
    title: string;
    duration: number; // Duration in weeks
    enrolledStudents: string[] = []; // Array to store enrolled students
```

```
// Constructor to initialize properties
constructor(title: string, duration: number) {
    this.title = title;
    this.duration = duration;
}


// Method to display course details
displayCourseInfo() {
    console.log(`Course Title: ${this.title}`);
    console.log(`Duration: ${this.duration} weeks`);
}


// Method to enroll a student
enrollStudent(studentName: string) {
    this.enrolledStudents.push(studentName);
    console.log(`${studentName} has been enrolled in ${this.title}.`);
}


// Method to display enrolled students
displayEnrolledStudents() {
    console.log(`Enrolled Students in ${this.title}:
```

```
${this.enrolledStudents.join(", ")}`);
    }
}


// Creating an instance of the Course class
const course3 = new Course("TypeScript Masterclass", 8);

// Enrolling students and displaying information
course3.enrollStudent("Alice");
course3.enrollStudent("Bob");
course3.displayCourseInfo();
course3.displayEnrolledStudents();
// Output:
// Alice has been enrolled in TypeScript Masterclass.
// Bob has been enrolled in TypeScript Masterclass.
// Course Title: TypeScript Masterclass
// Duration: 8 weeks
// Enrolled Students in TypeScript Masterclass: Alice, Bob
```

In the above code, the **Course** class includes additional methods: **enrollStudent** and **displayEnrolledStudents**. These methods manage the enrollment of students and display relevant information.

Public, Private, and Protected Modifiers

Access modifiers control the visibility and accessibility of class members. They determine how properties and methods can be accessed from outside the class.

Public Modifier

The **public** modifier allows class members to be accessed from anywhere. By default, all members are **public** unless specified otherwise.

```
// Using the public modifier

class Course {

    public title: string;

    public duration: number;

    public enrolledStudents: string[] = [];


    constructor(title: string, duration: number) {

        this.title = title;

        this.duration = duration;

    }


    public displayCourseInfo() {

        console.log(`Course Title: ${this.title}`);

        console.log(`Duration: ${this.duration} weeks`);

    }

}
```

In the above code, all class members are explicitly marked as **public**, indicating they can be accessed from outside the class.

Private Modifier

The **private** modifier restricts access to class members, allowing them to be accessed only within the class itself.

```
// Using the private modifier
class Course {
    private title: string;
    private duration: number;
    private enrolledStudents: string[] = [];

    constructor(title: string, duration: number) {
        this.title = title;
        this.duration = duration;
    }

    public displayCourseInfo() {
        console.log(`Course Title: ${this.title}`);
        console.log(`Duration: ${this.duration} weeks`);
    }

    public enrollStudent(studentName: string) {
        this.enrolledStudents.push(studentName);
```

```typescript
        console.log(`${studentName} has been enrolled in ${this.title}.`);
    }

    public displayEnrolledStudents() {
        console.log(`Enrolled Students in ${this.title}: ${this.enrolledStudents.join(", ")}`);
    }
}


// Creating an instance of the Course class
const course4 = new Course("TypeScript Masterclass", 8);


// Accessing private members (will result in an error)
// course4.title = "New Title"; // Error: Property 'title' is private and only accessible within class 'Course'.


// Using public methods to interact with private members
course4.enrollStudent("Alice");
course4.displayCourseInfo();
```

In the above code, the **title**, **duration**, and **enrolledStudents** properties are marked as **private**, preventing direct access from outside the class. Instead, public methods are used to interact with these private members.

Protected Modifier

The **protected** modifier allows access to class members within the class and its subclasses but not from outside.

```
// Using the protected modifier
class Course {
    protected title: string;
    protected duration: number;
    protected enrolledStudents: string[] = [];

    constructor(title: string, duration: number) {
        this.title = title;
        this.duration = duration;
    }

    protected displayCourseInfo() {
        console.log(`Course Title: ${this.title}`);
        console.log(`Duration: ${this.duration} weeks`);
    }
}

// Subclass of Course with additional functionality
class AdvancedCourse extends Course {
```

```typescript
    constructor(title: string, duration: number) {
        super(title, duration);
    }


    public displayAdvancedCourseInfo() {
        this.displayCourseInfo(); // Accessing protected method
        console.log(`This is an advanced course.`);
    }
}


// Creating an instance of the AdvancedCourse class
const advancedCourse = new AdvancedCourse("Advanced TypeScript", 6);


// Accessing protected members (will result in an error)
// console.log(advancedCourse.title); // Error: Property 'title' is protected and only accessible within class 'Course' and its subclasses.


// Using subclass methods to access protected members
advancedCourse.displayAdvancedCourseInfo();
// Output:
```

```
// Course Title: Advanced TypeScript
// Duration: 6 weeks
// This is an advanced course.
```

In the above code, the **title**, **duration**, and **enrolledStudents** properties and the **displayCourseInfo** method are marked as **protected**. They can be accessed within the **AdvancedCourse** subclass but not from outside the class hierarchy.

Sample Program

We will integrate these concepts into our ongoing project, "Anna's TS Coaching," to manage student and course data effectively.

```
// Class to represent a student
class Student {
    private id: number;
    public name: string;
    public courses: Course[] = [];

    constructor(id: number, name: string) {
        this.id = id;
        this.name = name;
    }

    public enrollInCourse(course: Course) {
        this.courses.push(course);
        course.enrollStudent(this.name);
```

```
    }

    public displayStudentInfo() {
        console.log(`Student ID: ${this.id}`);
        console.log(`Student Name: ${this.name}`);
        console.log(`Enrolled Courses: ${this.courses.map(course => course.title).join(", ")}`);
    }
}


// Creating students and enrolling them in courses
const student1 = new Student(1, "Alice");
const student2 = new Student(2, "Bob");

student1.enrollInCourse(course4);
student2.enrollInCourse(course4);

student1.displayStudentInfo();
student2.displayStudentInfo();
// Output:
// Student ID: 1
// Student Name: Alice
```

```
// Enrolled Courses: TypeScript Masterclass

// Student ID: 2

// Student Name: Bob

// Enrolled Courses: TypeScript Masterclass
```

In the above code, we create a **Student** class with a private **id** property and public methods to enroll in courses and display student information. We demonstrate how classes, constructors, methods, and access modifiers work together to manage student and course data in our project.

Class Inheritance and Modifiers

Class inheritance is a fundamental concept in object-oriented programming that allows you to create a new class based on an existing class. This enables you to extend and customize the behavior of existing classes, promoting code reuse and modularity. In TypeScript, you can use inheritance to build hierarchical class structures. Additionally, TypeScript provides abstract classes and access modifiers to further control class behavior and accessibility. We will explore these concepts and apply them to our project.

Implementing Inheritance

Inheritance allows a class (subclass) to inherit properties and methods from another class (superclass). The subclass can add or override methods and properties to provide specialized functionality.

We will create a base class **Person** and extend it with the **Student** and **Instructor** classes.

```
// Defining a base class Person

class Person {

    name: string;

    age: number;


    constructor(name: string, age: number) {

        this.name = name;
```

```
        this.age = age;
    }

    displayInfo() {
        console.log(`Name: ${this.name}, Age: ${this.age}`);
    }
}


// Extending the Person class with the Student class
class Student extends Person {
    courses: string[] = [];

    constructor(name: string, age: number) {
        super(name, age); // Call the constructor of the superclass
    }

    enroll(course: string) {
        this.courses.push(course);
        console.log(`${this.name} has enrolled in ${course}.`);
```

```
    }


    displayCourses() {
        console.log(`Enrolled Courses: ${this.courses.join(", ")}`);
    }
}


// Extending the Person class with the Instructor class
class Instructor extends Person {
    expertise: string;


    constructor(name: string, age: number, expertise: string) {
        super(name, age);
        this.expertise = expertise;
    }


    displayExpertise() {
        console.log(`${this.name} is an expert in ${this.expertise}.`);
    }
```

```typescript
}

// Creating instances of Student and Instructor
const student = new Student("Alice", 20);
const instructor = new Instructor("Bob", 35, "TypeScript");

student.enroll("TypeScript Basics");
student.displayInfo(); // Output: Name: Alice, Age: 20
student.displayCourses(); // Output: Enrolled Courses: TypeScript Basics

instructor.displayInfo(); // Output: Name: Bob, Age: 35
instructor.displayExpertise(); // Output: Bob is an expert in TypeScript
```

In the above code, the **Person** class is a base class with common properties **name** and **age**. The **Student** class inherits from **Person** and adds additional methods for course enrollment, while the **Instructor** class inherits from **Person** and adds expertise-related functionality. The **super** keyword is used to call the constructor of the superclass, allowing the **Student** and **Instructor** classes to initialize inherited properties.

Defining Abstract Classes

Abstract classes provide a way to define base classes that cannot be instantiated directly. They can contain abstract methods without implementation, which must be implemented by subclasses. Abstract classes allow you to define a common interface for derived classes while enforcing specific behavior.

We will create an abstract class **CourseMember** to represent a member of a course and use it as a base for **Student** and **Instructor** classes.

```typescript
// Defining an abstract class CourseMember
abstract class CourseMember {
    name: string;

    constructor(name: string) {
        this.name = name;
    }


    // Abstract method to display role-specific information
    abstract displayRoleInfo(): void;

    displayName() {
        console.log(`Name: ${this.name}`);
    }
}


// Extending the abstract class CourseMember with the Student class
class Student extends CourseMember {
    courses: string[] = [];
```

```
    constructor(name: string) {
        super(name);
    }

    enroll(course: string) {
        this.courses.push(course);
        console.log(`${this.name} has enrolled in ${course}.`);
    }

    displayCourses() {
        console.log(`Enrolled Courses: ${this.courses.join(", ")}`);
    }

    displayRoleInfo() {
        console.log(`${this.name} is a student.`);
    }
}

// Extending the abstract class CourseMember with the
```

Instructor class

```
class Instructor extends CourseMember {
    expertise: string;

    constructor(name: string, expertise: string) {
        super(name);
        this.expertise = expertise;
    }

    displayExpertise() {
        console.log(`${this.name} is an expert in ${this.expertise}.`);
    }

    displayRoleInfo() {
        console.log(`${this.name} is an instructor.`);
    }
}


// Creating instances of Student and Instructor
const student2 = new Student("Charlie");
const instructor2 = new Instructor("David", "Advanced
```

```
TypeScript");

student2.enroll("Advanced TypeScript");

student2.displayName(); // Output: Name: Charlie

student2.displayRoleInfo(); // Output: Charlie is a student.


instructor2.displayName(); // Output: Name: David

instructor2.displayRoleInfo(); // Output: David is an instructor.
```

In the above code, **CourseMember** is an abstract class with an abstract method **displayRoleInfo**. The **Student** and **Instructor** classes extend **CourseMember** and provide their implementations for **displayRoleInfo**, defining role-specific behavior.

Applying Access Modifiers in Inheritance

Access modifiers (**public**, **private**, **protected**) control the visibility and accessibility of class members in inheritance scenarios. They determine how properties and methods can be accessed from subclasses.

We will demonstrate how access modifiers affect class inheritance and member accessibility.

```
// Defining a base class Course
class Course {
    public title: string;
    protected duration: number;
    private enrolledStudents: string[] = [];
```

```typescript
    constructor(title: string, duration: number) {
        this.title = title;
        this.duration = duration;
    }

    public displayTitle() {
        console.log(`Course Title: ${this.title}`);
    }

    protected displayDuration() {
        console.log(`Course Duration: ${this.duration} weeks`);
    }

    private addStudent(studentName: string) {
        this.enrolledStudents.push(studentName);
    }

    public enroll(studentName: string) {
        this.addStudent(studentName);
        console.log(`${studentName} has enrolled in ${this.title}.`);
```

```typescript
    }
}

// Extending the Course class with AdvancedCourse
class AdvancedCourse extends Course {
    constructor(title: string, duration: number) {
        super(title, duration);
    }

    public displayCourseDetails() {
        this.displayTitle();
        this.displayDuration(); // Accessing protected method
    }
}

// Creating an instance of AdvancedCourse
const advancedCourse2 = new AdvancedCourse("Mastering TypeScript", 8);

advancedCourse2.displayCourseDetails();
// Output:
```

```
// Course Title: Mastering TypeScript
// Course Duration: 8 weeks
```

```
advancedCourse2.enroll("Eve");
// Output: Eve has enrolled in Mastering TypeScript
```

```
// Attempting to access private members (will result in an error)
// advancedCourse2.enrolledStudents.push("Eve"); // Error: Property 'enrolledStudents' is private and only accessible within class 'Course'.
```

In the above code, the **Course** class has a **public** property **title**, a **protected** property **duration**, and a **private** property **enrolledStudents**. The **AdvancedCourse** class extends **Course** and can access the **public** and **protected** members but not the **private** members. The **displayCourseDetails** method demonstrates how protected members can be accessed within subclasses.

Sample Program

We will integrate inheritance, abstract classes, and access modifiers into our project to manage course roles and information.

```
// Abstract class for course members
abstract class CourseMember {
    protected id: number;
    protected name: string;


    constructor(id: number, name: string) {
```

```typescript
        this.id = id;
        this.name = name;
    }

    abstract displayRoleInfo(): void;

    displayName() {
        console.log(`Name: ${this.name}`);
    }
}

// Student class extending CourseMember
class Student extends CourseMember {
    private courses: Course[] = [];

    constructor(id: number, name: string) {
        super(id, name);
    }

    public enroll(course: Course) {
        this.courses.push(course);
```

```typescript
        course.enroll(this.name);
    }

    public displayCourses() {
        console.log(`Enrolled Courses for ${this.name}: ${this.courses.map(course => course.title).join(", ")}`);
    }

    public displayRoleInfo() {
        console.log(`${this.name} is a student.`);
    }
}

// Instructor class extending CourseMember
class Instructor extends CourseMember {
    private expertise: string;

    constructor(id: number, name: string, expertise: string) {
        super(id, name);
        this.expertise = expertise;
    }
```

```
    public displayExpertise() {

        console.log(`${this.name} is an expert in ${this.expertise}.`);

    }


    public displayRoleInfo() {

        console.log(`${this.name} is an instructor.`);

    }
}


// Course class with access modifiers
class Course {

    public title: string;

    private enrolledStudents: string[] = [];


    constructor(title: string) {

        this.title = title;

    }


    public enroll(studentName: string) {

        this.enrolledStudents.push(studentName);
```

```
        console.log(`${studentName} has enrolled in ${this.title}.`);
    }


    public displayEnrolledStudents() {
        console.log(`Enrolled Students in ${this.title}: ${this.enrolledStudents.join(", ")}`);
    }
}


// Creating instances and demonstrating functionality
const course5 = new Course("TypeScript Fundamentals");

const student3 = new Student(1, "Fiona");
const instructor3 = new Instructor(2, "George", "JavaScript");

student3.enroll(course5);
student3.displayName(); // Output: Name: Fiona
student3.displayRoleInfo(); // Output: Fiona is a student.
student3.displayCourses(); // Output: Enrolled Courses for Fiona: TypeScript Fundamentals
```

```
instructor3.displayName(); // Output: Name: George

instructor3.displayRoleInfo(); // Output: George is an
instructor.

instructor3.displayExpertise(); // Output: George is an
expert in JavaScript


course5.displayEnrolledStudents(); // Output: Enrolled
Students in TypeScript Fundamentals: Fiona
```

In the above code, we use abstract classes and inheritance to manage course roles in our project. The **CourseMember** abstract class serves as a base for **Student** and **Instructor** classes, while access modifiers control the visibility and accessibility of class members.

Interfaces in Action

Interfaces define a contract that a class or object must adhere to. They specify the structure of an object, including the properties and methods it should have, without providing any implementation. This allows for consistent and interchangeable use of objects and classes that implement the interface. Interfaces can also include optional and readonly properties, providing flexibility and control over object structures.

Defining an Interface

To define an interface, use the **interface** keyword followed by the interface name and the structure it should enforce. Classes can then implement these interfaces using the **implements** keyword, ensuring they adhere to the defined structure.

We will define interfaces for **CourseMember** and **Course** to represent the structure of these entities in our project.

```
// Defining an interface for CourseMember

interface ICourseMember {
    id: number;
```

```
    name: string;

    displayRoleInfo(): void;

}


// Defining an interface for Course

interface ICourse {

    title: string;

    enroll(studentName: string): void;

    displayEnrolledStudents(): void;

}
```

In the above code, **ICourseMember** defines the structure for a course member with an **id**, **name**, and a method **displayRoleInfo**. Similarly, **ICourse** defines the structure for a course with a **title** and methods for enrolling students and displaying enrolled students.

Implementing Interfaces in Classes

We will implement these interfaces in the **Student**, **Instructor**, and **Course** classes.

```
// Implementing the ICourseMember interface in the Student class

class Student implements ICourseMember {

    id: number;

    name: string;

    private courses: ICourse[] = [];

    constructor(id: number, name: string) {
```

```
        this.id = id;

        this.name = name;

    }


    enroll(course: ICourse) {

        this.courses.push(course);

        course.enroll(this.name);

    }


    displayCourses() {

        console.log(`Enrolled Courses for ${this.name}: ${this.courses.map(course => course.title).join(", ")}`);

    }


    displayRoleInfo() {

        console.log(`${this.name} is a student.`);

    }

}


// Implementing the ICourseMember interface in the Instructor class

class Instructor implements ICourseMember {
```

```typescript
    id: number;

    name: string;

    private expertise: string;


    constructor(id: number, name: string, expertise: string) {

        this.id = id;

        this.name = name;

        this.expertise = expertise;

    }


    displayExpertise() {

        console.log(`${this.name} is an expert in ${this.expertise}.`);

    }


    displayRoleInfo() {

        console.log(`${this.name} is an instructor.`);

    }

}


// Implementing the ICourse interface in the Course class
```

```typescript
class Course implements ICourse {
    title: string;
    private enrolledStudents: string[] = [];

    constructor(title: string) {
        this.title = title;
    }

    enroll(studentName: string) {
        this.enrolledStudents.push(studentName);
        console.log(`${studentName} has enrolled in ${this.title}.`);
    }

    displayEnrolledStudents() {
        console.log(`Enrolled Students in ${this.title}: ${this.enrolledStudents.join(", ")}`);
    }
}

// Creating instances and demonstrating functionality
const course6: ICourse = new Course("TypeScript
```

```
Fundamentals");

const student4: ICourseMember = new Student(1, "Henry");

const instructor4: ICourseMember = new Instructor(2, "Irene", "TypeScript");


student4.displayRoleInfo(); // Output: Henry is a student.

student4.enroll(course6); // Output: Henry has enrolled in TypeScript Fundamentals.

(course6 as Course).displayEnrolledStudents(); // Output: Enrolled Students in TypeScript Fundamentals: Henry


instructor4.displayRoleInfo(); // Output: Irene is an instructor.

(instructor4 as Instructor).displayExpertise(); // Output: Irene is an expert in TypeScript
```

In the above code, the **Student** and **Instructor** classes implement the **ICourseMember** interface, ensuring they have the required properties and methods. The **Course** class implements the **ICourse** interface, providing the necessary methods for managing course enrollment.

Optional Properties

Optional properties in interfaces allow for properties that may or may not be present in an object. They are defined using the question mark (**?**) after the property name.

We will update the **ICourse** interface to include an optional **description** property.

```
// Updating the ICourse interface with an optional property
```

```typescript
interface ICourse {
    title: string;
    description?: string; // Optional property
    enroll(studentName: string): void;
    displayEnrolledStudents(): void;
}


// Implementing the ICourse interface with an optional property
class Course implements ICourse {
    title: string;
    description?: string;
    private enrolledStudents: string[] = [];

    constructor(title: string, description?: string) {
        this.title = title;
        this.description = description;
    }

    enroll(studentName: string) {
        this.enrolledStudents.push(studentName);
        console.log(`${studentName} has enrolled in
```

```
${this.title}.`);
    }


    displayEnrolledStudents() {
        console.log(`Enrolled Students in ${this.title}: ${this.enrolledStudents.join(", ")}`);
    }


    displayCourseDetails() {
        console.log(`Course Title: ${this.title}`);
        if (this.description) {
            console.log(`Description: ${this.description}`);
        } else {
            console.log("No description available.");
        }
    }
}

// Creating an instance with an optional property
const course7 = new Course("TypeScript Advanced Course", "An in-depth look at TypeScript.");
course7.displayCourseDetails(); // Output includes
```

description

```
const course8 = new Course("TypeScript Basics");
course8.displayCourseDetails(); // Output indicates no description
```

In the above code, the **ICourse** interface includes an optional **description** property. The **Course** class implements this interface and checks for the presence of the **description** property, displaying it if available.

Readonly Properties

Readonly properties in interfaces are properties that cannot be modified after they are initialized. They are defined using the **readonly** keyword before the property name.

We will update the **ICourseMember** interface to include a readonly **id** property.

```
// Updating the ICourseMember interface with a readonly property
interface ICourseMember {
    readonly id: number; // Readonly property
    name: string;
    displayRoleInfo(): void;
}


// Implementing the ICourseMember interface with a readonly property
class Student implements ICourseMember {
    readonly id: number;
```

```typescript
    name: string;

    private courses: ICourse[] = [];

    constructor(id: number, name: string) {
        this.id = id;
        this.name = name;
    }

    enroll(course: ICourse) {
        this.courses.push(course);
        course.enroll(this.name);
    }

    displayCourses() {
        console.log(`Enrolled Courses for ${this.name}: ${this.courses.map(course => course.title).join(", ")}`);
    }

    displayRoleInfo() {
        console.log(`${this.name} is a student.`);
    }
}
```

```
// Attempting to modify a readonly property (will result 
in an error)

const student5 = new Student(3, "Jenna");

console.log(`Student ID: ${student5.id}`); // Output: 
Student ID: 3


// student5.id = 4; // Error: Cannot assign to 'id' 
because it is a read-only property.
```

In the above code, the **ICourseMember** interface includes a readonly **id** property, ensuring that once a student's ID is set, it cannot be changed. The **Student** class implements this interface, demonstrating the use of readonly properties.

Sample Program

We will apply interfaces, optional properties, and readonly properties to our project, enhancing the structure and consistency of our application.

```
// Interface for Course with optional and readonly 
properties

interface ICourse {

    title: string;

    description?: string;

    enroll(studentName: string): void;

    displayEnrolledStudents(): void;

}
```

```typescript
// Interface for CourseMember with readonly properties
interface ICourseMember {
    readonly id: number;
    name: string;
    displayRoleInfo(): void;
}


// Student class implementing ICourseMember
class Student implements ICourseMember {
    readonly id: number;
    name: string;
    private courses: ICourse[] = [];

    constructor(id: number, name: string) {
        this.id = id;
        this.name = name;
    }

    enroll(course: ICourse) {
        this.courses.push(course);
```

```
        course.enroll(this.name);
    }


    displayCourses() {
        console.log(`Enrolled Courses for ${this.name}: ${this.courses.map(course => course.title).join(", ")}`);
    }


    displayRoleInfo() {
        console.log(`${this.name} is a student.`);
    }
}


// Instructor class implementing ICourseMember
class Instructor implements ICourseMember {
    readonly id: number;
    name: string;
    private expertise: string;


    constructor(id: number, name: string, expertise: string) {
        this.id = id;
```

```
        this.name = name;
        this.expertise = expertise;
    }


    displayExpertise() {
        console.log(`${this.name} is an expert in ${this.expertise}.`);
    }


    displayRoleInfo() {
        console.log(`${this.name} is an instructor.`);
    }
}


// Course class implementing ICourse
class Course implements ICourse {
    title: string;
    description?: string;
    private enrolledStudents: string[] = [];


    constructor(title: string, description?: string) {
        this.title = title;
```

```
        this.description = description;

    }


    enroll(studentName: string) {

        this.enrolledStudents.push(studentName);

        console.log(`${studentName} has enrolled in ${this.title}.`);

    }


    displayEnrolledStudents() {

        console.log(`Enrolled Students in ${this.title}: ${this.enrolledStudents.join(", ")}`);

    }


    displayCourseDetails() {

        console.log(`Course Title: ${this.title}`);

        if (this.description) {

            console.log(`Description: ${this.description}`);

        } else {

            console.log("No description available.");

        }
```

```typescript
    }
}

// Creating instances and demonstrating functionality

const course9 = new Course("TypeScript Mastery", "A comprehensive course on TypeScript.");

const student6 = new Student(4, "Kyle");

const instructor5 = new Instructor(5, "Liam", "JavaScript");


student6.enroll(course9);

student6.displayCourses(); // Output: Enrolled Courses for Kyle: TypeScript Mastery


instructor5.displayRoleInfo(); // Output: Liam is an instructor.

instructor5.displayExpertise(); // Output: Liam is an expert in JavaScript


course9.displayCourseDetails(); // Output includes course description

course9.displayEnrolledStudents(); // Output: Enrolled Students in TypeScript Mastery: Kyle
```

In the above code, interfaces are used to define the structure of course and course member objects, ensuring consistency and adherence to a common contract. Optional and readonly properties provide flexibility and control over object structures, enhancing the robustness of our project.

Extending Interfaces

In TypeScript, interfaces can be extended to create more complex and hierarchical structures. This allows you to build upon existing interfaces and combine them to define new types, making your code more modular and flexible. Extending interfaces can help manage complexity by breaking down large interfaces into smaller, more manageable pieces.

Extending Interfaces

When you extend an interface, you create a new interface that inherits all properties and methods from one or more existing interfaces. This is done using the **extends** keyword.

Extending a Single Interface

We will extend the **ICourseMember** interface to create a more specific interface for students, including additional properties and methods.

```
// Extending the ICourseMember interface for students
interface IStudent extends ICourseMember {
    courses: ICourse[]; // Property to store enrolled courses
    enroll(course: ICourse): void; // Method to enroll in a course
    displayCourses(): void; // Method to display enrolled courses
}


// Implementing the extended IStudent interface in the Student class
```

```typescript
class Student implements IStudent {
    readonly id: number;
    name: string;
    courses: ICourse[] = [];

    constructor(id: number, name: string) {
        this.id = id;
        this.name = name;
    }

    enroll(course: ICourse) {
        this.courses.push(course);
        course.enroll(this.name);
    }


    displayCourses() {
        console.log(`Enrolled Courses for ${this.name}: ${this.courses.map(course => course.title).join(", ")}`);
    }


    displayRoleInfo() {
        console.log(`${this.name} is a student.`);
```

```typescript
        }
    }

    // Creating an instance of the Student class
    const student7 = new Student(6, "Olivia");

    student7.enroll(new Course("TypeScript Essentials"));
    student7.displayRoleInfo(); // Output: Olivia is a student.
    student7.displayCourses(); // Output: Enrolled Courses for Olivia: TypeScript Essentials
```

In the above code, the **IStudent** interface extends **ICourseMember** to include additional properties and methods specific to students. The **Student** class implements **IStudent**, adhering to the contract defined by both **ICourseMember** and **IStudent**.

Extending Multiple Interfaces

You can also extend multiple interfaces at once to combine properties and methods from various sources into a single interface.

```typescript
// Extending ICourse and ICourseMember interfaces for a combined role
interface IInstructor extends ICourseMember {
    expertise: string;
    displayExpertise(): void;
}
```

```
// Implementing the extended IInstructor interface in the Instructor class

class Instructor implements IInstructor {

    readonly id: number;

    name: string;

    expertise: string;


    constructor(id: number, name: string, expertise: string) {

        this.id = id;

        this.name = name;

        this.expertise = expertise;

    }


    displayExpertise() {

        console.log(`${this.name} is an expert in ${this.expertise}.`);

    }


    displayRoleInfo() {

        console.log(`${this.name} is an instructor.`);

    }
```

}

```
// Creating an instance of the Instructor class
const instructor6 = new Instructor(7, "Emma", "React");
```

```
instructor6.displayRoleInfo(); // Output: Emma is an instructor.

instructor6.displayExpertise(); // Output: Emma is an expert in React
```

In the above code, the **IInstructor** interface extends **ICourseMember** to include properties and methods specific to instructors. The **Instructor** class implements **IInstructor**, ensuring it adheres to the contract defined by both interfaces.

Combining Interfaces with Intersection Types

Combining interfaces allows you to create new interfaces by merging properties and methods from multiple interfaces. This can be useful when you want to represent a composite type that involves multiple roles or responsibilities.

We will combine the **IStudent** and **IInstructor** interfaces to represent a teaching assistant (TA) role that includes both student and instructor responsibilities.

```
// Defining an interface for a Teaching Assistant
interface ITeachingAssistant extends IStudent, IInstructor {
    assistWithCourse(course: ICourse): void; // Method to assist with a course
}
```

```typescript
// Implementing the ITeachingAssistant interface in the TeachingAssistant class
class TeachingAssistant implements ITeachingAssistant {
    readonly id: number;
    name: string;
    courses: ICourse[] = [];
    expertise: string;

    constructor(id: number, name: string, expertise: string) {
        this.id = id;
        this.name = name;
        this.expertise = expertise;
    }

    enroll(course: ICourse) {
        this.courses.push(course);
        course.enroll(this.name);
    }

    displayCourses() {
        console.log(`Enrolled Courses for ${this.name}:
```

```typescript
${this.courses.map(course => course.title).join(", ")}`);
    }

    displayRoleInfo() {
        console.log(`${this.name} is a teaching assistant.`);
    }

    displayExpertise() {
        console.log(`${this.name} is knowledgeable in ${this.expertise}.`);
    }

    assistWithCourse(course: ICourse) {
        console.log(`${this.name} is assisting with the course: ${course.title}.`);
    }
}

// Creating an instance of the TeachingAssistant class
const ta = new TeachingAssistant(8, "Sophia", "TypeScript");
```

```
ta.enroll(new Course("TypeScript Advanced Concepts"));

ta.displayRoleInfo(); // Output: Sophia is a teaching assistant.

ta.displayCourses(); // Output: Enrolled Courses for Sophia: TypeScript Advanced Concepts

ta.displayExpertise(); // Output: Sophia is knowledgeable in TypeScript

ta.assistWithCourse(new Course("React Basics")); // Output: Sophia is assisting with the course: React Basics
```

In the above code, the **ITeachingAssistant** interface combines **IStudent** and **IInstructor**, creating a composite interface that represents a teaching assistant. The **TeachingAssistant** class implements this interface, ensuring it fulfills the responsibilities of both a student and an instructor.

Sample Program

We will apply interface extension and combination to our project, creating flexible and comprehensive type definitions for various roles.

```
// Interface for Course with optional and readonly properties

interface ICourse {

    title: string;

    description?: string;

    enroll(studentName: string): void;

    displayEnrolledStudents(): void;

}
```

```typescript
// Interface for CourseMember with readonly properties
interface ICourseMember {
    readonly id: number;
    name: string;
    displayRoleInfo(): void;
}


// Interface for Student extending CourseMember
interface IStudent extends ICourseMember {
    courses: ICourse[];
    enroll(course: ICourse): void;
    displayCourses(): void;
}


// Interface for Instructor extending CourseMember
interface IInstructor extends ICourseMember {
    expertise: string;
    displayExpertise(): void;
}


// Interface for Teaching Assistant combining Student and Instructor
```

```typescript
interface ITeachingAssistant extends IStudent,
IInstructor {
    assistWithCourse(course: ICourse): void;
}


// Course class implementing ICourse
class Course implements ICourse {
    title: string;
    description?: string;
    private enrolledStudents: string[] = [];

    constructor(title: string, description?: string) {
        this.title = title;
        this.description = description;
    }

    enroll(studentName: string) {
        this.enrolledStudents.push(studentName);
        console.log(`${studentName} has enrolled in ${this.title}.`);
    }
```

```typescript
    displayEnrolledStudents() {
        console.log(`Enrolled Students in ${this.title}: ${this.enrolledStudents.join(", ")}`);
    }


    displayCourseDetails() {
        console.log(`Course Title: ${this.title}`);
        if (this.description) {
            console.log(`Description: ${this.description}`);
        } else {
            console.log("No description available.");
        }
    }
}


// Student class implementing IStudent
class Student implements IStudent {
    readonly id: number;
    name: string;
    courses: ICourse[] = [];
```

```typescript
    constructor(id: number, name: string) {
        this.id = id;
        this.name = name;
    }

    enroll(course: ICourse) {
        this.courses.push(course);
        course.enroll(this.name);
    }

    displayCourses() {
        console.log(`Enrolled Courses for ${this.name}: ${this.courses.map(course => course.title).join(", ")}`);
    }

    displayRoleInfo() {
        console.log(`${this.name} is a student.`);
    }
}

// Instructor class implementing IInstructor
class Instructor implements IInstructor {
```

```typescript
    readonly id: number;
    name: string;
    expertise: string;

    constructor(id: number, name: string, expertise: string) {
        this.id = id;
        this.name = name;
        this.expertise = expertise;
    }

    displayExpertise() {
        console.log(`${this.name} is an expert in ${this.expertise}.`);
    }

    displayRoleInfo() {
        console.log(`${this.name} is an instructor.`);
    }
}

// TeachingAssistant class implementing
```

ITeachingAssistant

```typescript
class TeachingAssistant implements ITeachingAssistant {
    readonly id: number;
    name: string;
    courses: ICourse[] = [];
    expertise: string;

    constructor(id: number, name: string, expertise: string) {
        this.id = id;
        this.name = name;
        this.expertise = expertise;
    }

    enroll(course: ICourse) {
        this.courses.push(course);
        course.enroll(this.name);
    }

    displayCourses() {
        console.log(`Enrolled Courses for ${this.name}: ${this.courses.map(course => course.title).join(", ")}`);
```

```typescript
    }

    displayRoleInfo() {
        console.log(`${this.name} is a teaching assistant.`);
    }

    displayExpertise() {
        console.log(`${this.name} is knowledgeable in ${this.expertise}.`);
    }

    assistWithCourse(course: ICourse) {
        console.log(`${this.name} is assisting with the course: ${course.title}.`);
    }
}

// Creating instances and demonstrating functionality

const course10 = new Course("Advanced TypeScript", "Deep dive into TypeScript.");

const student8 = new Student(9, "Liam");

const instructor7 = new Instructor(10, "Noah",
```

```
"TypeScript");
const ta2 = new TeachingAssistant(11, "Ava",
"JavaScript");


student8.enroll(course10);
student8.displayCourses(); // Output: Enrolled Courses
for Liam: Advanced TypeScript


instructor7.displayRoleInfo(); // Output: Noah is an
instructor.
instructor7.displayExpertise(); // Output: Noah is an
expert in TypeScript


ta2.enroll(course10);
ta2.displayCourses(); // Output: Enrolled Courses for
Ava: Advanced TypeScript
ta2.displayRoleInfo(); // Output: Ava is a teaching
assistant.
ta2.displayExpertise(); // Output: Ava is knowledgeable
in JavaScript
ta2.assistWithCourse(new Course("React Basics")); //
Output: Ava is assisting with the course: React Basics


course10.displayEnrolledStudents(); // Output: Enrolled
Students in Advanced TypeScript: Liam, Ava
```

In the above code, we demonstrate how to extend and combine interfaces to create complex and flexible type definitions. By applying these concepts to our project, we ensure that various roles and responsibilities are clearly defined and consistently implemented.

Summary

In Chapter 5, we delved into the core object-oriented features of TypeScript, focusing on classes and interfaces to enhance code organization, modularity, and reusability. We began by exploring the definition and use of classes, learning how to create classes with properties, constructors, and methods to encapsulate data and behavior effectively. This section introduced the use of access modifiers, such as **`public`**, **`private`**, and **`protected`**, to control the visibility and accessibility of class members, thereby ensuring data encapsulation and security.

We then moved on to class inheritance, understanding how to create hierarchical structures by extending classes. This allowed us to reuse and extend existing functionality, enhancing code maintainability. The concept of abstract classes was introduced, which provided a blueprint for subclasses to implement, allowing for the definition of common interfaces with enforced behaviors. We implemented these concepts in our project to model various roles, such as students and instructors, demonstrating the power of inheritance and abstraction.

The chapter also covered interfaces, a key feature in TypeScript for defining contracts that classes must adhere to. We explored how to implement interfaces in classes, ensuring consistency across implementations and enabling flexible code that can adapt to different needs. Interfaces with optional and readonly properties were learned, providing control over which properties are required and which can be modified.

Finally, we learned about extending and combining interfaces to create more complex and flexible type definitions. This allowed us to manage intricate roles and responsibilities within our project, ensuring a clear and consistent implementation of different roles, such as teaching assistants who combine the features of students and instructors. By the end of this chapter, we had developed a robust understanding of how to utilize classes and interfaces to build scalable and maintainable applications.

Chapter 6: Modules and Namespaces

Chapter Overview

We will start with chapter 6. In this chapter, we go further into TypeScript's module and namespace concepts. Modules and namespaces provide structure and encapsulation, allowing for clear separation of different parts of a program. We will start with an introduction to modules, learning how they allow us to divide code into reusable and maintainable chunks. Modules improve the separation of concerns, making it easier to manage dependencies and share code between projects.

Next, we will look at how modules are imported and exported. This section will demonstrate how to use TypeScript's module system to import external modules and export your own, allowing for seamless integration of various code components. We will look at the differences between default and named exports, and learn when and how to use them to improve code efficiency and clarity. We will also learn about using namespaces, which provide another way to organize code. Namespaces enable you to group related functionalities and avoid naming conflicts, especially in large applications. We will look at how namespaces differ from modules and when they are most useful, especially in situations where module bundlers are not used.

Finally, we will cover module resolution and configuration, which are critical for understanding how TypeScript resolves module paths and dependencies. This section will go over the configuration options in the tsconfig.json file that can be used to optimize the module resolution process, such as paths and base URLs. Once you finish this chapter, you will know everything there is to know about modules and namespaces, and you will be able to organize TypeScript projects like a pro.

Introduction to Modules

Modules provide a way to encapsulate code, making it more modular and maintainable. In TypeScript, modules are based on the ECMAScript 6 (ES6) module system, which has become the standard for JavaScript modules. This system allows developers to define and use modules across projects, ensuring code is organized, reusable, and easy to understand.

Module Structure

Modules are files that encapsulate a set of related functionalities. Each module can contain classes, functions, variables, or any other piece of code that makes up a specific feature or set of features. By using modules, developers can break their applications into smaller, logical components that can be developed, tested, and maintained independently. This separation of concerns allows for cleaner code and reduces the complexity of managing large codebases.

In TypeScript, each file is treated as a separate module. This is true for any file that contains import or export statements. Modules can export any of their declarations, such as variables, functions, classes, interfaces, or type aliases, making them available for use in other modules.

Consider a simple example of a module:

```typescript
// mathUtils.ts - A module exporting mathematical utilities

export function add(a: number, b: number): number {
    return a + b;
}


export function subtract(a: number, b: number): number {
    return a - b;
}


export const PI = 3.14159;
```

In the above code, the **mathUtils.ts** file exports two functions, **add** and **subtract**, as well as a constant **PI**. These exports make the module's functionalities available to other modules that import them.

Module Working in ES6

The ES6 module system is a built-in feature of JavaScript that allows you to import and export code between files. It provides a standardized way to include code from one module in another, enabling developers to create modular applications.

To make code available from a module, you use the **export** keyword. There are several ways to export code in ES6:

Named Exports

Named exports allow you to export multiple values from a module by name. You can have multiple named exports in a single module.

```typescript
// mathUtils.ts
```

```typescript
export function multiply(a: number, b: number): number {
    return a * b;
}
```

```typescript
export const EULER = 2.71828;
```

In the above code, the **mathUtils.ts** module exports a function **multiply** and a constant **EULER** as named exports.

Default Exports

Default exports allow you to export a single value from a module. This value is the module's "default" export, and each module can have only one default export.

```typescript
// config.ts

export default {
    appName: "Anna's TS Coaching",
    version: "1.0.0",
    debugMode: true
};
```

In the above code, the **config.ts** module exports an object as the default export, representing the application's configuration.

Exporting Declarations

You can also export declarations directly when defining them:

```typescript
// geometry.ts

export class Circle {
    constructor(public radius: number) {}
```

```typescript
    getArea(): number {
        return Math.PI * this.radius * this.radius;
    }
}

export function calculateCircumference(radius: number): number {
    return 2 * Math.PI * radius;
}
```

Here, the **Circle** class and the **calculateCircumference** function are exported as part of the **geometry.ts** module.

Now, to use code from another module, you import it using the **import** keyword. There are several ways to import code in ES6:

Named Imports

Named imports allow you to import specific exports by name. This method is used when you want to import multiple named exports.

```typescript
// main.ts
import { add, subtract, PI } from './mathUtils';

console.log(add(5, 3)); // Output: 8
console.log(`Value of PI: ${PI}`); // Output: Value of PI: 3.14159
```

In the above code, the **main.ts** module imports the **add** and **subtract** functions, as well as the **PI** constant, from the **mathUtils.ts** module.

Default Imports

Default imports allow you to import a module's default export. This method is used when you want to import a module's default export, which can be named anything during import.

```
// appConfig.ts

import config from './config';


console.log(`App Name: ${config.appName}`); // Output: App Name: Anna's TS Coaching
```

In the above code, the **appConfig.ts** module imports the default export from the **config.ts** module and uses it to access the application's configuration.

Importing All as Object

You can import all exports from a module as a single object using the * as syntax.

```
// shapes.ts

import * as Geometry from './geometry';


const circle = new Geometry.Circle(5);

console.log(`Circle Area: ${circle.getArea()}`); // Output: Circle Area: 78.53975
```

Here, the **shapes.ts** module imports all exports from the **geometry.ts** module as a single object named **Geometry**, allowing access to its members.

Working of Modules

TypeScript builds upon the ES6 module system by adding static type checking, enhancing the development experience. TypeScript modules allow developers to define types and interfaces alongside their code, ensuring that module boundaries are respected and type-safe.

We will see a complete example of how modules work in a TypeScript project.

Defining Modules

```typescript
// student.ts - A module defining a Student class
export class Student {
    constructor(public id: number, public name: string, public courses: string[] = []) {}

    enroll(course: string) {
        this.courses.push(course);
        console.log(`${this.name} has enrolled in ${course}.`);
    }

    displayCourses() {
        console.log(`Enrolled Courses for ${this.name}: ${this.courses.join(", ")}`);
    }
}

// instructor.ts - A module defining an Instructor class
export class Instructor {
    constructor(public id: number, public name: string, public expertise: string) {}
```

```
    displayExpertise() {
        console.log(`${this.name} is an expert in ${this.expertise}.`);
    }
}
```

Putting Modules into Use

```
// app.ts - Main application file importing and using modules
import { Student } from './student';
import { Instructor } from './instructor';


const student = new Student(1, "Alice");
const instructor = new Instructor(2, "Bob", "TypeScript");


student.enroll("TypeScript Basics");
student.displayCourses(); // Output: Enrolled Courses for Alice: TypeScript Basics


instructor.displayExpertise(); // Output: Bob is an expert in TypeScript
```

In the above code, the **student.ts** and **instructor.ts** files define modules with the

Student and **Instructor** classes, respectively. The `app.ts` file imports these modules and uses their functionalities, demonstrating how modules allow for clean and organized code.

Importing and Exporting Modules

In TypeScript, the ability to import and export modules is essential for creating organized, scalable, and maintainable codebases. By splitting your code into modules, you can separate concerns, manage dependencies, and reuse code across different parts of an application. In this section, we will delve deeper into the mechanisms for importing and exporting modules, building upon what we learned in the previous topic. We will also explore how to alias imports, providing more control over how you use and refer to module exports.

Exporting Modules

Exporting code from a module makes it accessible to other modules. TypeScript supports several ways to export code, each serving different purposes. Here, we will explore the main types of exports: named exports, default exports, and export lists.

Named Exports

Named exports allow you to export multiple values from a module. Each exported value is explicitly named, enabling you to export several variables, functions, or classes.

```
// utilities.ts - A module exporting named utilities

export function formatDate(date: Date): string {
    return date.toISOString().split('T')[0];
}


export const appName = "Anna's TS Coaching";


export class Logger {
    log(message: string) {
        console.log(`[${new Date().toISOString()}]
```

```
${message}`);
    }
}
```

In the above code, the **utilities.ts** module exports a function **formatDate**, a constant **appName**, and a class **Logger** as named exports. This allows other modules to import these exports by name.

Default Exports

Default exports allow you to export a single value from a module as its default export. This is useful when a module is expected to export only one main entity.

```
// config.ts - A module with a default export
export default {
    appName: "Anna's TS Coaching",
    version: "1.0.0",
    debugMode: true
};
```

Here, the **config.ts** module exports an object as its default export, representing the application's configuration. Default exports are ideal for modules that have a primary focus or purpose.

Exporting Declarations

You can also export declarations directly when defining them, making it clear which items are intended to be public.

```
// math.ts - A module exporting mathematical functions
export function add(a: number, b: number): number {
    return a + b;
}
```

```typescript
export function multiply(a: number, b: number): number {
    return a * b;
}
```

In the above code, the **math.ts** module exports the **add** and **multiply** functions directly upon definition, making them available for import in other modules.

Export Lists

You can group exports into an export list, providing a clear overview of what is exported from a module.

```typescript
// shapes.ts - A module using an export list
function calculateCircleArea(radius: number): number {
    return Math.PI * radius * radius;
}


function calculateSquareArea(side: number): number {
    return side * side;
}


export { calculateCircleArea, calculateSquareArea };
```

In the above code, the **shapes.ts** module uses an export list to export the **calculateCircleArea** and **calculateSquareArea** functions, enhancing readability and organization.

Importing Modules

Importing modules allows you to use code from other modules within your own. TypeScript provides several ways to import exports, including named imports, default imports, and importing everything as an object.

Named Imports

Named imports allow you to import specific exports by name. This method is ideal when you need to import multiple named exports from a module.

```typescript
// main.ts - Importing named exports
import { formatDate, appName, Logger } from './utilities';

const logger = new Logger();
logger.log(`Welcome to ${appName}`); // Output: [timestamp] Welcome to Anna's TS Coaching

const today = new Date();
console.log(`Today's date is ${formatDate(today)}`); // Output: Today's date is YYYY-MM-DD
```

In the above code, the **main.ts** module imports the **formatDate** function, **appName** constant, and **Logger** class from the **utilities.ts** module as named imports. This allows the **main.ts** module to use these utilities in its code.

Default Imports

Default imports allow you to import a module's default export. This method is used when a module has a primary export that serves as its main functionality.

```typescript
// appConfig.ts - Importing a default export
import config from './config';
```

```
console.log(`App Name: ${config.appName}`); // Output:
App Name: Anna's TS Coaching

console.log(`App Version: ${config.version}`); // Output:
App Version: 1.0.0
```

In the above code, the **appConfig.ts** module imports the default export from the **config.ts** module, using it to access the application's configuration properties.

Import as Object

You can import all exports from a module as a single object using the *** as** syntax. This method is useful when you want to access all exports under a single namespace.

```
// geometry.ts - Importing all exports as an object
import * as MathUtils from './math';


console.log(`Sum: ${MathUtils.add(3, 5)}`); // Output:
Sum: 8

console.log(`Product: ${MathUtils.multiply(4, 6)}`); //
Output: Product: 24
```

In the above code, the **geometry.ts** module imports all exports from the **math.ts** module as a single object named **MathUtils**, allowing access to its members using dot notation.

Aliasing Imports

Alias imports allow you to rename imports when importing them, providing flexibility and avoiding naming conflicts. This can be particularly useful when two modules have exports with the same name.

Alias for Named Imports

You can alias named imports by using the **as** keyword.

```
// logger.ts - Importing with aliases
```

```
import { Logger as AppLogger, formatDate as format } from
'./utilities';

const logger = new AppLogger();

logger.log('Application started'); // Output: [timestamp]
Application started


const date = new Date();

console.log(`Formatted Date: ${format(date)}`); //
Output: Formatted Date: YYYY-MM-DD
```

In the above code, the **logger.ts** module imports the **Logger** class and **formatDate** function from the **utilities.ts** module using aliases **AppLogger** and **format**, respectively. This allows for more readable code and avoids conflicts with other imports.

Alias for Default Imports

Although default imports can be named anything, you can still use aliasing to clarify intent or resolve conflicts.

```
// settings.ts - Importing a default export with an alias

import appConfig from './config';


console.log(`Debug Mode: ${appConfig.debugMode}`); //
Output: Debug Mode: true
```

In the above code, the **settings.ts** module imports the default export from the **config.ts** module with the name **appConfig**, which serves as an alias for clarity. Similarly, you may proceed to apply all these concepts by organizing various functionalities into modules and using imports and exports to integrate them.

Combining Default and Named Exports

In many cases, you may find it beneficial to combine default and named exports within a single module. This approach allows you to provide a primary export while still offering additional named utilities or constants that complement the main functionality.

We will explore how to combine default and named exports in the context of a course management module within our project.

Following is the quick sample program:

```
// courseManager.ts - A module with default and named exports


// Named export: Course class
export class Course {
    constructor(public title: string, public description?: string) {}


    displayCourseInfo() {
        console.log(`Course Title: ${this.title}`);
        if (this.description) {
            console.log(`Description: ${this.description}`);
        } else {
            console.log("No description available.");
        }
    }
}
```

```typescript
}


// Named export: Utility function
export function getCourseDetails(course: Course): string {
    return `Course: ${course.title} - ${course.description ?? "No description"}`;
}


// Named export: Constant
export const DEFAULT_COURSE_TITLE = "Untitled Course";


// Default export: CourseManager class
export default class CourseManager {
    private courses: Course[] = [];

    addCourse(course: Course) {
        this.courses.push(course);
        console.log(`Course "${course.title}" added.`);
    }

    listCourses() {
```

```
        console.log("Courses:");
        this.courses.forEach((course, index) => {
            console.log(`${index + 1}. ${getCourseDetails(course)}`);
        });
    }
}
```

In the above code, the **courseManager.ts** module exports a **Course** class, a **getCourseDetails** utility function, and a **DEFAULT_COURSE_TITLE** constant as named exports. Additionally, it exports a **CourseManager** class as the default export. The default export serves as the main functionality of the module, while the named exports provide supporting utilities and constants.

Now, let's see how to import and use both default and named exports from the **courseManager.ts** module.

```
// main.ts - Importing and using default and named exports


// Importing named exports
import { Course, DEFAULT_COURSE_TITLE } from './courseManager';


// Importing the default export with an alias
import CourseManager from './courseManager';


// Creating instances of Course and CourseManager
```

```
const courseManager = new CourseManager();

const course1 = new Course("TypeScript Basics", "Introduction to TypeScript");
const course2 = new Course(DEFAULT_COURSE_TITLE); // Using the default title

// Adding courses using the CourseManager
courseManager.addCourse(course1);
courseManager.addCourse(course2);

// Listing all courses
courseManager.listCourses();

// Output:
// Course "TypeScript Basics" added.
// Course "Untitled Course" added.
// Courses:
// 1. Course: TypeScript Basics - Introduction to TypeScript
// 2. Course: Untitled Course - No description
```

In the above code, the **main.ts** file imports the **Course** class and **DEFAULT_COURSE_TITLE** constant as named imports and the **CourseManager** class as a default import. The use of both import types allows the module to be used flexibly, accessing both the primary functionality and supplementary utilities. Each module combines default and named exports to provide a structured and flexible codebase. The **main.ts** file demonstrates how to import and use these modules to manage different aspects of the coaching application, showcasing the benefits of combining default and named exports in a modular application.

Working with Namespaces

Namespaces are a way to organize code and avoid naming conflicts by providing a logical grouping of related functionalities. They allow you to encapsulate code within a named container, which can be particularly useful in large projects where many modules and components need to coexist without interfering with each other. While modules are the preferred approach in modern TypeScript development, namespaces can still be valuable for specific scenarios, especially when working without module bundlers. In this topic, we will learn how to define namespaces and use nested namespaces within our project.

Defining Namespaces

Namespaces are defined using the **namespace** keyword, followed by the namespace name. Within a namespace, you can define classes, functions, interfaces, variables, and other TypeScript constructs. By encapsulating these elements within a namespace, you prevent naming conflicts and enhance code organization.

Creating a Namespace

We will start by defining a namespace for utility functions and constants used in our project.

```typescript
// utilities.ts - Defining a namespace for utilities


namespace Utilities {

    export function formatDate(date: Date): string {

        return date.toISOString().split('T')[0];

    }


    export const appName = "Anna's TS Coaching";
```

```
    export class Logger {
        log(message: string) {
            console.log(`[${new Date().toISOString()}] ${message}`);
        }
    }
}
```

In the above code, the **Utilities** namespace encapsulates a function **formatDate**, a constant **appName**, and a class **Logger**. By using the **export** keyword, these elements are made accessible outside the namespace.

Using a Namespace

To use the elements defined within a namespace, you reference them using the namespace name as a prefix.

```
// main.ts - Using the Utilities namespace


/// <reference path="utilities.ts" />


const logger = new Utilities.Logger();

logger.log(`Welcome to ${Utilities.appName}`); // Output: [timestamp] Welcome to Anna's TS Coaching


const today = new Date();

console.log(`Today's date is
```

```
${Utilities.formatDate(today)}`); // Output: Today's date
is YYYY-MM-DD
```

In the above code, the **main.ts** file uses the **Utilities** namespace by referencing its path with a **/// <reference path="utilities.ts" />** directive. The **Logger** class and **formatDate** function are accessed using the **Utilities** prefix.

Nested Namespaces

Namespaces can be nested within other namespaces, allowing you to create a hierarchical organization of related functionalities. Nested namespaces are useful for organizing complex projects with multiple levels of abstraction.

Creating Nested Namespaces

We will define a namespace for a module that deals with geometry calculations, nesting it within a parent namespace.

```
// geometry.ts - Defining a parent namespace with nested
namespaces



namespace MathUtils {

    export namespace Geometry {

        export function calculateCircleArea(radius:
number): number {

            return Math.PI * radius * radius;

        }


        export function calculateSquareArea(side:
number): number {

            return side * side;

        }
```

```
    }

    export namespace Algebra {
        export function solveLinearEquation(a: number, b: number): number {
            if (a === 0) throw new Error("No solution for a = 0");
            return -b / a;
        }
    }
}
```

In the above code, the **MathUtils** namespace serves as the parent namespace, containing two nested namespaces: **Geometry** and **Algebra**. Each nested namespace encapsulates specific functionalities related to its domain.

Using Nested Namespaces

To access elements within nested namespaces, you use the full namespace path as a prefix.

```
// calculations.ts - Using the MathUtils namespace


/// <reference path="geometry.ts" />


const radius = 5;
console.log(`Circle Area: ${MathUtils.Geometry.calculateCircleArea(radius)}`); // Output: Circle Area: 78.53981633974483
```

```
const side = 4;

console.log(`Square Area: ${MathUtils.Geometry.calculateSquareArea(side)}`); // Output: Square Area: 16


const solution = MathUtils.Algebra.solveLinearEquation(2, -8);

console.log(`Solution to the equation 2x - 8 = 0 is x = ${solution}`); // Output: Solution to the equation 2x - 8 = 0 is x = 4
```

In the above code, the **calculations.ts** file uses the **MathUtils** namespace and its nested namespaces **Geometry** and **Algebra**. The calculations for circle and square areas, as well as solving a linear equation, are performed using the corresponding functions from the nested namespaces.

Sample Program

We will apply namespaces to our project to organize different parts of the application.

Defining Namespaces for Project Components

Namespace for Student Management

```
// student.ts - Defining a namespace for student management


namespace AnnaCoaching {
    export namespace StudentModule {
        export class Student {
```

```
        constructor(public id: number, public name: 
string, public courses: Course[] = []) {}

            enroll(course: Course) {
                this.courses.push(course);
                console.log(`${this.name} has enrolled in 
${course.title}.`);
            }

            displayCourses() {
                console.log(`Enrolled Courses for 
${this.name}: ${this.courses.map(course => 
course.title).join(", ")}`);
            }
        }
    }
}
```

Namespace for Instructor Management

```
// instructor.ts - Defining a namespace for instructor 
management

namespace AnnaCoaching {
    export namespace InstructorModule {
```

```typescript
export class Instructor {
    constructor(public id: number, public name: string, public expertise: string) {}

    displayExpertise() {
        console.log(`${this.name} is an expert in ${this.expertise}.`);
    }
  }
 }
}
```

Namespace for Course Management

```typescript
// course.ts - Defining a namespace for course management

namespace AnnaCoaching {
    export namespace CourseModule {
        export class Course {
            constructor(public title: string, public description?: string) {}

            displayCourseInfo() {
                console.log(`Course Title: ${this.title}`);
```

```typescript
            if (this.description) {
                console.log(`Description: ${this.description}`);
            } else {
                console.log("No description available.");
            }
        }
    }
}
```

Using Namespaces in the Project

```typescript
// main.ts - Using namespaces in the project

/// <reference path="student.ts" />
/// <reference path="instructor.ts" />
/// <reference path="course.ts" />

const course = new AnnaCoaching.CourseModule.Course("TypeScript Mastery", "In-depth TypeScript training");

const student = new AnnaCoaching.StudentModule.Student(1, "Liam");
```

```
const instructor = new
AnnaCoaching.InstructorModule.Instructor(2, "Sophia",
"JavaScript");
```

```
student.enroll(course);
```

```
student.displayCourses(); // Output: Enrolled Courses for
Liam: TypeScript Mastery
```

```
instructor.displayExpertise(); // Output: Sophia is an
expert in JavaScript
```

```
course.displayCourseInfo();
// Output:
// Course Title: TypeScript Mastery
// Description: In-depth TypeScript training
```

In the above code, we organized the components of our project into namespaces, each encapsulating related functionalities for students, instructors, and courses. The **main.ts** file demonstrates how to use these namespaces to manage different aspects of the coaching application, showcasing the benefits of namespaces in creating a well-structured and maintainable project.

Summary

Finally, we had a look at TypeScript's modules and namespaces, with an emphasis on how they help with code organization and management in bigger applications. The chapter began with an overview of modules, emphasizing how they allow developers to encapsulate code into reusable and maintainable pieces. We looked at the ES6 module system, which TypeScript is built upon, and learned how to export and import code between files. The discussion of named and default exports shed light on how developers can manage the core functionality of modules as well as supplementary utilities. By combining default and named exports, we demonstrated how to create modular applications with clear separation of concerns and code flexibility.

The chapter went on to teach namespaces, which provide an alternative way to structure code that is particularly useful in scenarios without module bundlers. We defined namespaces to encapsulate related functionalities and avoid naming conflicts, thereby improving code readability and organization. The introduction of nested namespaces enabled us to understand hierarchical structures for larger projects. Using practical examples from our project, we used namespaces to organize the various aspects of the coaching application, including student, instructor, and course management.

Finally, we learned module resolution and configuration, specifically how TypeScript resolves module paths and dependencies. The chapter explained how to configure the tsconfig.json file to optimize module resolution, ensure efficient integration, and manage project dependencies.

Chapter 7: TypeScript in Practice

Chapter Overview

Here we will look at several real-world uses of TypeScript, such as migrating from JavaScript to TypeScript and integrating it with popular front-end frameworks and tools. We will start by looking at how TypeScript can be combined with Angular, a popular framework for developing strong online apps. We may improve the development time, code quality, and scalability of the application by utilizing TypeScript's static typing and capabilities.

Next, we will look at how TypeScript can be integrated with React, a popular user interface toolkit. TypeScript's type-checking features can greatly help React projects by improving tools support and minimizing runtime errors. We will show you how to set up a React project with TypeScript and how it can speed up component development while improving overall code readability. This integration will also highlight TypeScript's advantages for sustaining huge React apps. The chapter will also go over the process of transitioning existing JavaScript apps to TypeScript. This transition allows teams to gradually adopt TypeScript's benefits rather than rebuilding entire codebases from scratch. We will walk you through the necessary stages for a smooth transfer, identifying potential problems and demonstrating how to handle them efficiently.

Finally, we will look at how to test TypeScript applications, highlighting the need of designing dependable tests to ensure code accuracy and stability. We will explain common TypeScript-compatible testing frameworks and tools, as well as demonstrate how to set up and run tests for various areas of an application.

Integrating TypeScript with Angular

Angular is a popular framework for building dynamic and robust web applications. One of Angular's key features is its integration with TypeScript, which provides static typing and powerful tools to enhance the development experience. In this topic, we will explore how to set up an Angular project with TypeScript and how to utilize TypeScript within Angular components and services. By doing so, we will unlock the full potential of TypeScript's features to create efficient, scalable, and maintainable Angular applications.

Setting up Angular Project

To begin using TypeScript in an Angular project, we need to set up a new Angular application using the Angular CLI, a command-line interface tool that streamlines the process of creating and managing Angular projects.

Installing Angular CLI

First, ensure that you have Node.js and npm installed on your system. You can verify this by running the following commands:

```
node -v

npm -v
```

Once Node.js and npm are installed, you can install the Angular CLI globally by running:

```
npm install -g @angular/cli
```

This command installs the Angular CLI, which you can use to generate a new Angular project.

Creating a New Angular Project

To create a new Angular project, run the following command:

```
ng new anna-ts-coaching
```

The CLI will prompt you to answer a few questions about your project setup. Select the default options, and ensure TypeScript is the selected language, as Angular projects are TypeScript-based by default. The CLI will then generate a new project named **anna-ts-coaching**.

Once the project is created, navigate to the project directory:

```
cd anna-ts-coaching
```

Running the Angular Project

Start the Angular development server with the following command:

```
ng serve
```

The Angular CLI will compile the application and launch a development server at **http://localhost:4200/**. Open this URL in your browser to view the running Angular application.

Utilizing TypeScript in Angular Components

In Angular, components are the building blocks of the user interface. They are responsible for rendering the view and handling user interactions. TypeScript plays a crucial role in defining components by providing static typing, interfaces, and decorators.

Creating an Angular Component

To create a new Angular component, use the Angular CLI's **generate** command:

```
ng generate component student-list
```

This command generates a new component named **StudentListComponent** in the **src/app/student-list/** directory. The component consists of four files:

- **student-list.component.ts**: TypeScript file defining the component logic.
- **student-list.component.html**: HTML template for the component's view.
- **student-list.component.css**: CSS styles for the component.
- **student-list.component.spec.ts**: Unit test file for the component.

Defining a Component with TypeScript

We will explore the generated **student-list.component.ts** file:

```typescript
// student-list.component.ts

import { Component } from '@angular/core';


@Component({
  selector: 'app-student-list',
  templateUrl: './student-list.component.html',
  styleUrls: ['./student-list.component.css']
})
export class StudentListComponent {
  students: { id: number; name: string; }[] = [
    { id: 1, name: 'Liam' },
    { id: 2, name: 'Sophia' },
    { id: 3, name: 'Olivia' }
  ];
```

```
  constructor() {}

  addStudent(id: number, name: string): void {
    this.students.push({ id, name });
  }
}
```

In the above code, we define a **StudentListComponent** class decorated with the **@Component** decorator. The decorator specifies the component's selector, template, and styles. The **students** property is an array of student objects, each with an **id** and **name**. TypeScript's type annotations ensure that the **students** array is strictly typed, preventing errors.

The **addStudent** method adds a new student to the array, illustrating how TypeScript can provide type safety and improved development experience within components.

Using Component in Angular Templates

To use the **StudentListComponent** in the application, add its selector to the **app.component.html** file:

```
<!-- app.component.html -->


<h1>Welcome to Anna's TS Coaching!</h1>

<app-student-list></app-student-list>
```

When you reload the application, the **StudentListComponent** will be rendered, displaying the list of students.

Utilizing TypeScript in Angular Services

Services in Angular are used to encapsulate business logic and shared functionalities. They are typically used to manage data, handle HTTP requests, and perform operations that need to be shared across components. TypeScript's features, such as interfaces and decorators, enhance the development and organization of Angular services.

Creating an Angular Service

To create a new Angular service, use the Angular CLI's **generate** command:

```
ng generate service student
```

This command generates a new service named **StudentService** in the **src/app/student/** directory. The service consists of a single file:

- **student.service.ts**: TypeScript file defining the service logic.

Defining a Service with TypeScript

We will explore the generated **student.service.ts** file and add some logic:

```typescript
// student.service.ts


import { Injectable } from '@angular/core';


interface Student {
  id: number;
  name: string;
}


@Injectable({
  providedIn: 'root'
})
export class StudentService {
```

```
  private students: Student[] = [
    { id: 1, name: 'Liam' },
    { id: 2, name: 'Sophia' },
    { id: 3, name: 'Olivia' }
  ];

  constructor() {}

  getStudents(): Student[] {
    return this.students;
  }

  addStudent(student: Student): void {
    this.students.push(student);
  }
}
```

In the above code, we define a **StudentService** class decorated with the **@Injectable** decorator, indicating that this service can be injected into other components and services. The **students** array is defined as a private property, encapsulating the student data within the service. The **Student** interface defines the shape of student objects, providing type safety when handling student data.

The **getStudents** method returns the list of students, while the **addStudent** method adds a new student to the array. TypeScript's static typing and interfaces enhance the service by enforcing correct usage of data structures and methods.

Using the Service in Angular Components

To use the **StudentService** in a component, inject it into the component's constructor and use its methods.

```ts
// student-list.component.ts

import { Component, OnInit } from '@angular/core';
import { StudentService } from '../student/student.service';

@Component({
  selector: 'app-student-list',
  templateUrl: './student-list.component.html',
  styleUrls: ['./student-list.component.css']
})
export class StudentListComponent implements OnInit {
  students: { id: number; name: string; }[] = [];

  constructor(private studentService: StudentService) {}

  ngOnInit(): void {
    this.students = this.studentService.getStudents();
  }
```

```
  addStudent(id: number, name: string): void {

    this.studentService.addStudent({ id, name });

    this.students = this.studentService.getStudents(); // Refresh the list

  }

}
```

In the above code, the **StudentService** is injected into the **StudentListComponent** through the constructor, allowing the component to access the service's methods. The **ngOnInit** lifecycle hook initializes the **students** array by calling **getStudents** from the service. The **addStudent** method adds a new student using the service and refreshes the list by fetching the updated student data.

Integrating TypeScript with Angular Features

Angular's rich ecosystem provides various features that seamlessly integrate with TypeScript, enhancing the development process and code quality.

TypeScript in Angular Directives

Directives in Angular are classes that add behavior to elements in the DOM. TypeScript's type annotations and decorators enhance the creation and management of directives.

```
// highlight.directive.ts


import { Directive, ElementRef, Renderer2, HostListener } from '@angular/core';


@Directive({
  selector: '[appHighlight]'
```

```
})
export class HighlightDirective {

  constructor(private el: ElementRef, private renderer: Renderer2) {}


  @HostListener('mouseenter') onMouseEnter() {

    this.renderer.setStyle(this.el.nativeElement, 'background-color', 'yellow');

  }


  @HostListener('mouseleave') onMouseLeave() {

    this.renderer.setStyle(this.el.nativeElement, 'background-color', 'transparent');

  }

}
```

In the above code, we define a **HighlightDirective** that changes the background color of an element when the mouse enters and leaves. The directive uses the **@Directive** decorator to specify its selector and TypeScript's type annotations to manage dependencies like **ElementRef** and **Renderer2**. The **@HostListener** decorator is used to bind methods to DOM events.

Using TypeScript with Angular Pipes

Pipes in Angular transform data before it is displayed in the view. TypeScript enhances pipes by providing type safety and improved tooling support.

```
// capitalize.pipe.ts
```

```
import { Pipe, PipeTransform } from '@angular/core';

@Pipe({
  name: 'capitalize'
})
export class CapitalizePipe implements PipeTransform {
  transform(value: string): string {
    if (!value) return '';
    return value.charAt(0).toUpperCase() + value.slice(1).toLowerCase();
  }
}
```

In the above code, we define a **CapitalizePipe** that capitalizes the first letter of a string. The pipe uses the **@Pipe** decorator to specify its name and implements the **PipeTransform** interface to define its transformation logic. TypeScript ensures that the **transform** method adheres to the correct signature, providing consistency and reliability.

Integrating TypeScript with React

React is a powerful library for building user interfaces, and integrating TypeScript with React can significantly enhance your development experience. TypeScript provides static typing, improved tooling, and better code quality, making React applications more robust and maintainable. In this topic, we will explore how to set up a React project with TypeScript and utilize TypeScript features within React components, hooks, and context.

Setting up React with TypeScript

To begin using TypeScript in a React project, you can use Create React App (CRA), a tool that sets up a modern React application with minimal configuration. CRA supports TypeScript out of the box, making it easy to get started.

First, open the terminal and run the following command to create a new React project with TypeScript:

```
npx create-react-app anna-ts-coaching --template typescript
```

This command generates a new React project named **anna-ts-coaching** with TypeScript configuration. Navigate to the project directory:

```
cd anna-ts-coaching
```

Start the React development server with the following command:

```
npm start
```

The development server will compile the application and open it in your default browser at **http://localhost:3000/**.

Utilizing TypeScript in React Components

React components are the building blocks of React applications. TypeScript enhances component development by providing static typing for props, state, and other component properties.

Defining a Functional Component with TypeScript

We will create a functional component to display a list of students. For this, first create a new component file, called as StudentList.tsx

```
// src/components/StudentList.tsx


import React, { useState } from 'react';


// Define the shape of student objects using an interface
interface Student {
    id: number;
```

```
  name: string;
}


// Define the props interface for the component
interface StudentListProps {
  initialStudents: Student[];
}


const StudentList: React.FC<StudentListProps> = ({ initialStudents }) => {
  const [students, setStudents] = useState<Student[]>(initialStudents);


  // Function to add a new student
  const addStudent = (name: string) => {
    const newStudent: Student = { id: students.length + 1, name };
    setStudents([...students, newStudent]);
  };


  return (
    <div>
```

```
      <h2>Student List</h2>
      <ul>
        {students.map(student => (
          <li key={student.id}>{student.name}</li>
        ))}
      </ul>
      <button onClick={() => addStudent('New Student')}>Add Student</button>
    </div>
  );
};
```

`export default StudentList;`

In the above code, we define a **StudentList** component using the **React.FC** type to indicate that it is a functional component. We use TypeScript interfaces to define the shape of student objects and the props the component expects. The **useState** hook is used to manage the list of students, with TypeScript ensuring that the state and related functions adhere to the defined types.

Using the Component in the Application

Add the **StudentList** component to the **App.tsx** file:

`// src/App.tsx`

`import React from 'react';`

`import StudentList from './components/StudentList';`

```
// Initial student data
const initialStudents = [
  { id: 1, name: 'Liam' },
  { id: 2, name: 'Sophia' },
  { id: 3, name: 'Olivia' }
];

const App: React.FC = () => {
  return (
    <div>
      <h1>Welcome to Anna's TS Coaching!</h1>
      <StudentList initialStudents={initialStudents} />
    </div>
  );
};

export default App;
```

In the above code, the **App** component imports and uses the **StudentList** component, passing the **initialStudents** array as a prop. TypeScript ensures that the prop type matches the expected shape, providing type safety and improved development experience.

Utilizing TypeScript with React Hooks

React hooks are functions that let you use state and lifecycle features in functional components. TypeScript enhances hooks by providing type safety and clarity.

Using TypeScript with useState Hook

We've already seen an example of using TypeScript with the useState hook in the StudentList component. We will further explore how TypeScript works with hooks by creating a custom hook to manage student data. For this, let us first create a new hook file: useStudentManager.ts

```
// src/hooks/useStudentManager.ts


import { useState } from 'react';


// Define the shape of student objects using an interface
interface Student {
   id: number;
   name: string;
}


export const useStudentManager = (initialStudents: Student[]) => {
   const [students, setStudents] = useState<Student[]>(initialStudents);

   const addStudent = (name: string) => {
     const newStudent: Student = { id: students.length +
```

```
1, name };
    setStudents([...students, newStudent]);
  };


  const removeStudent = (id: number) => {
    setStudents(students.filter(student => student.id !== id));
  };


  return { students, addStudent, removeStudent };
};
```

In the above code, the **useStudentManager** hook manages a list of students, providing functions to add and remove students. TypeScript ensures that the hook's state and functions are correctly typed, enhancing code reliability.

Using Custom Hook in Component

Update the **StudentList** component to use the **useStudentManager** hook:

```
// src/components/StudentList.tsx


import React from 'react';
import { useStudentManager } from '../hooks/useStudentManager';


// Define the shape of student objects using an interface
```

```typescript
interface Student {
  id: number;
  name: string;
}

// Define the props interface for the component
interface StudentListProps {
  initialStudents: Student[];
}

const StudentList: React.FC<StudentListProps> = ({ initialStudents }) => {
  const { students, addStudent, removeStudent } = useStudentManager(initialStudents);

  return (
    <div>
      <h2>Student List</h2>
      <ul>
        {students.map(student => (
          <li key={student.id}>
            {student.name}
```

```
            <button onClick={() =>
removeStudent(student.id)}>Remove</button>

        </li>

    ))}

    </ul>

        <button onClick={() => addStudent('New
Student')}>Add Student</button>

    </div>

  );

};


export default StudentList;
```

In this updated example, the **StudentList** component uses the **useStudentManager** hook to manage student data. The hook provides the state and functions needed to add and remove students, demonstrating how TypeScript enhances hooks with type safety.

Utilizing TypeScript with React Context

React Context provides a way to pass data through the component tree without manually passing props at every level. TypeScript can enhance Context by providing clear types for the data and functions it manages.

Creating a Context with TypeScript

We will create a context to manage the theme of the application with a new context file: ThemeContext.tsx

```
// src/context/ThemeContext.tsx


import React, { createContext, useContext, useState }
```

```
from 'react';

// Define the shape of the theme context data
interface ThemeContextType {
  theme: string;
  toggleTheme: () => void;
}


// Create a context with an initial value
const ThemeContext = createContext<ThemeContextType | undefined>(undefined);


export const ThemeProvider: React.FC = ({ children }) => {
  const [theme, setTheme] = useState<string>('light');

  const toggleTheme = () => {
    setTheme(prevTheme => (prevTheme === 'light' ? 'dark' : 'light'));
  };

  return (
    <ThemeContext.Provider value={{ theme, toggleTheme
```

```
}}>
      {children}
    </ThemeContext.Provider>
  );
};


// Custom hook to use the ThemeContext
export const useTheme = (): ThemeContextType => {
  const context = useContext(ThemeContext);
  if (!context) {
    throw new Error('useTheme must be used within a ThemeProvider');
  }
  return context;
};
```

In the above code, we define a **ThemeContext** with a **theme** state and a **toggleTheme** function. The **ThemeProvider** component wraps the application, providing the theme context to its children. The **useTheme** hook provides a convenient way to access the theme context data, ensuring it is used correctly.

Using the Context in a Component

Update the **App** component to use the **ThemeContext**:

```
// src/App.tsx
```

```jsx
import React from 'react';
import StudentList from './components/StudentList';
import { ThemeProvider, useTheme } from './context/ThemeContext';

// Initial student data
const initialStudents = [
  { id: 1, name: 'Liam' },
  { id: 2, name: 'Sophia' },
  { id: 3, name: 'Olivia' }
];

// Theme toggle button component
const ThemeToggleButton: React.FC = () => {
  const { theme, toggleTheme } = useTheme();

  return (
    <button onClick={toggleTheme}>
      Switch to {theme === 'light' ? 'dark' : 'light'} mode
    </button>
  );
```

```
};

const App: React.FC = () => {
  return (
    <ThemeProvider>
      <div>
        <h1>Welcome to Anna's TS Coaching!</h1>
        <ThemeToggleButton />
        <StudentList initialStudents={initialStudents} />
      </div>
    </ThemeProvider>
  );
};

export default App;
```

In the above code, the **App** component wraps its children in the **ThemeProvider**, making the theme context available to the **ThemeToggleButton** component. The **ThemeToggleButton** uses the **useTheme** hook to access and toggle the theme, demonstrating how TypeScript and React Context work together to manage application-wide state.

Migrating JavaScript Applications to TypeScript

Migrating a JavaScript application to TypeScript can bring numerous benefits, including improved code quality, better tooling support, and enhanced maintainability. However, the migration process requires careful planning and execution to ensure a smooth transition. In this topic, we will outline a proven step-by-step process to migrate JavaScript applications to TypeScript and provide troubleshooting advice for common issues that may arise during the migration.

Migration Process

Migrating a JavaScript application to TypeScript involves several stages, from setting up TypeScript in your project to gradually converting JavaScript files. Given below is a step-by-step practical walkthrough to help you navigate this process.

Prepare the Project

Before starting the migration, ensure that your project is in a stable state and that you have a complete backup. This precaution will help you revert to the original code if needed.

- Ensure that your project dependencies are up-to-date.
- Remove any unused or deprecated libraries.
- Resolve any existing bugs or issues.

Install TypeScript

Add TypeScript to your project as a development dependency using npm or yarn.

```
# Using npm

npm install --save-dev typescript



# Using yarn

yarn add --dev typescript
```

Initialize TypeScript Configuration

Create a **tsconfig.json** file in your project root directory to configure TypeScript settings.

```
npx tsc --init
```

This command generates a default **tsconfig.json** file, which you can customize according to your project's needs. Key configurations to consider:

- **target**: Specify the JavaScript version (e.g., **"es6"**).
- **module**: Define the module system (e.g., **"commonjs"** or **"esnext"**).

- **`strict`**: Enable strict type-checking options for better type safety.
- **`include`**: Define which files or directories to include (e.g., `"src/**/*"`).
- **`exclude`**: Define files or directories to exclude (e.g., `"node_modules"`).

Rename JavaScript Files

Begin migrating files by renaming them from `.js` to `.ts`. Start with simpler, isolated files to minimize potential issues.

```
mv src/example.js src/example.ts
```

TypeScript can compile JavaScript files, so you can rename them incrementally, ensuring that the application continues to work.

Enable Type Checking

Run the TypeScript compiler (`tsc`) to enable type checking on the renamed files.

```
npx tsc
```

The TypeScript compiler will report any type errors or issues, allowing you to address them before proceeding.

Add Type Annotations

Gradually add type annotations to your TypeScript files to improve type safety and code readability.

- Annotate function parameters and return types.
- Define interfaces or type aliases for complex data structures.
- Use TypeScript's built-in types like `string`, `number`, and `boolean`.

Check the following example to understand the add type annotation:

```
// Before migration (JavaScript)
function greet(name) {
  return "Hello, " + name;
}
```

```
// After migration (TypeScript)
function greet(name: string): string {
    return "Hello, " + name;
}
```

Migrate Complex Files

Move on to more complex files, such as those with classes, interfaces, or external dependencies. Gradually replace JavaScript-specific constructs with TypeScript equivalents. See the following code to understand migrating a class.

```
// Before migration (JavaScript)
class Person {
    constructor(name) {
        this.name = name;
    }

    sayHello() {
        console.log(`Hello, my name is ${this.name}`);
    }
}

// After migration (TypeScript)
class Person {
```

```
  name: string;

  constructor(name: string) {
    this.name = name;
  }

  sayHello(): void {
    console.log(`Hello, my name is ${this.name}`);
  }
}
```

Address Third-Party Libraries

For third-party libraries that lack TypeScript definitions, you can install type definitions from DefinitelyTyped or create your own type declarations.

```
# Install type definitions for a library
npm install --save-dev @types/library-name
```

If no type definitions are available, you can create a **d.ts** file to define your own.

```
// custom-types.d.ts
declare module 'library-name' {
  export function someFunction(param: string): void;
}
```

Update Project Configuration

Once the migration is complete, update build scripts, linters, and IDE settings to ensure they

support TypeScript.
- Update **package.json** scripts to use **tsc** for compilation.
- Configure linters like ESLint to work with TypeScript.
- Ensure your IDE is set up to handle TypeScript files.

Troubleshooting Common Migration Issues

Despite careful planning, you may encounter challenges during the migration process. Given below are some common issues and potential solutions:

Compilation Errors

Think that the typeScript compilation fails with errors. Now, to solve it, we will address each error by refining type annotations, fixing type mismatches, or resolving dependencies.

The following is the example error on the Type Mismatch:

```
// Error: Type 'number' is not assignable to type 'string'.

let name: string = 123;

// Solution

let name: string = 'John';
```

Missing Type Definitions

Let us say that the third-party libraries lack TypeScript definitions. To resolve it, we install type definitions from DefinitelyTyped or we may create custom type declarations as shown below:

```
npm install --save-dev @types/lodash
```

Type Inference Issues

Let us say that the typeScript is unable to infer types correctly. Now, to address it, we will explicitly define types using annotations or interfaces in order to walkthrough you the TypeScript's inference.

```
// Without annotations

const add = (a, b) => a + b;
```

```
// With annotations
const add = (a: number, b: number): number => a + b;
```

Runtime Errors

Very commonly, the TypeScript fails or is not able to catch most of the runtime errors. In order to prevent this from happening, I would rather recommend to conduct thorough testing to catch issues that TypeScript's static analysis might miss. You must implement runtime checks for critical code paths as below:

```
function divide(a: number, b: number): number {
    if (b === 0) {
        throw new Error('Division by zero');
    }
    return a / b;
}
```

Implementing Migration

We will apply the migration process to a hypothetical JavaScript component from our project. Let us consider that the **course.js** is the original java script component as below:

```
// course.js


function Course(title, description) {
    this.title = title;
    this.description = description;
}
```

```
Course.prototype.displayInfo = function() {
  console.log('Course:', this.title);
  if (this.description) {
    console.log('Description:', this.description);
  } else {
    console.log('No description available.');
  }
};


const course = new Course('TypeScript Basics', 'Learn the basics of TypeScript.');
course.displayInfo();
```

And, the migrated typeScript component is course.ts

```
// course.ts

class Course {
  title: string;
  description?: string;

  constructor(title: string, description?: string) {
    this.title = title;
    this.description = description;
```

```
  }


  displayInfo(): void {
    console.log('Course:', this.title);
    if (this.description) {
      console.log('Description:', this.description);
    } else {
      console.log('No description available.');
    }
  }
}


const course = new Course('TypeScript Basics', 'Learn the basics of TypeScript.');

course.displayInfo();
```

In the above code, we migrated a simple JavaScript component to TypeScript by renaming the file and adding type annotations. We defined the **title** property as a string and the **description** property as an optional string, using TypeScript's type system to ensure correct data handling.

Through careful planning and execution, migrating JavaScript applications to TypeScript can unlock the benefits of type safety, improved tooling, and enhanced maintainability, leading to a more robust and reliable codebase. By following the outlined steps and troubleshooting advice, you can ensure a smooth transition and harness the full potential of TypeScript in your projects.

Testing TypeScript Applications

Overview

Testing is a critical aspect of software development that ensures the reliability and stability of applications. In TypeScript applications, testing helps verify that the code behaves as expected and identifies potential issues before they reach production. In this section, we will learn the different elements of an application that are typically tested, introduce and set up the Jest testing framework, and demonstrate how to write unit and integration test scripts.

When testing TypeScript applications, several key elements are typically evaluated to ensure the application functions correctly:

- Functions and methods are the core logic units of an application. Testing them verifies that they produce the expected output for a given input and handle edge cases appropriately.
- In component-based frameworks like Angular and React, components are tested to ensure they render correctly, handle user interactions, and manage state properly.
- Services encapsulate business logic and interact with external resources. Testing services ensure that they perform their intended operations and handle errors gracefully.
- APIs and endpoints are tested to verify that they return the expected data, handle requests correctly, and manage errors. This testing is crucial for applications that rely on external data sources.
- Testing user interfaces ensures that the application's visual elements are displayed correctly, respond to user actions, and maintain a consistent user experience.
- Integration testing evaluates how different parts of an application work together. This includes testing the interaction between components, services, and APIs.

Introduction to Jest

Jest is a popular testing framework for JavaScript and TypeScript applications. It provides a simple and efficient way to write and run tests, with built-in support for test runners, assertions, and mocking. Jest is well-suited for both unit and integration testing, making it a versatile choice for TypeScript projects.

Setting up Jest

To set up Jest for a TypeScript project, first add Jest and the necessary TypeScript support packages to your project as development dependencies:

```
npm install --save-dev jest ts-jest @types/jest
```

Here in the above code,
- **jest**: The core Jest testing framework.
- **ts-jest**: A TypeScript preprocessor for Jest, enabling it to run TypeScript tests.
- **@types/jest**: Type definitions for Jest, providing TypeScript support for Jest's API.

Configure Jest

Create a **jest.config.js** file in the project root directory to configure Jest settings:

```js
module.exports = {
  preset: 'ts-jest',
  testEnvironment: 'node',
  testPathIgnorePatterns: ['/node_modules/', '/dist/'],
  moduleFileExtensions: ['ts', 'tsx', 'js', 'jsx'],
  transform: {
    '^.+\\.(ts|tsx)$': 'ts-jest',
  },
};
```

This configuration specifies that Jest should use **ts-jest** to transform TypeScript files and run tests in a Node.js environment.

Add Jest Scripts

Update the **package.json** file to include a test script for running Jest tests:

```json
{
  "scripts": {
    "test": "jest"
  }
}
```

You can now run tests using the following command:

```
npm test
```

Writing Unit Test Scripts

Unit tests focus on testing individual functions or methods to verify their correctness in isolation. Jest provides a simple API for writing unit tests. Now, let's write unit tests for a utility function that formats dates through the utility function file **dateUtils.ts**

```typescript
// src/utils/dateUtils.ts

export function formatDate(date: Date): string {
  const year = date.getFullYear();
  const month = (date.getMonth() + 1).toString().padStart(2, '0');
  const day = date.getDate().toString().padStart(2, '0');
  return `${year}-${month}-${day}`;
}
```

Then, create the test file **dateUtils.test.ts**

```typescript
// src/utils/dateUtils.test.ts

import { formatDate } from './dateUtils';

describe('formatDate', () => {
```

```
  it('should format the date correctly', () => {
    const date = new Date(2024, 7, 1); // August 1, 2024
    const formattedDate = formatDate(date);
    expect(formattedDate).toBe('2024-08-01');
  });

  it('should handle single-digit months and days', () => {
    const date = new Date(2024, 0, 9); // January 9, 2024
    const formattedDate = formatDate(date);
    expect(formattedDate).toBe('2024-01-09');
  });
});
```

In the above code, we define a **formatDate** function in **dateUtils.ts** and write unit tests for it in **dateUtils.test.ts**. The tests verify that the function formats dates correctly and handles single-digit months and days. The **describe** block groups related tests, and the **it** blocks define individual test cases. The **expect** function is used to make assertions about the function's output.

Writing Integration Test Scripts

Integration tests evaluate how different parts of an application work together. They ensure that components interact correctly and produce the expected behavior.

We will write integration tests for a service that manages students. And for this, we will create the service file **studentService.ts**

```
// src/services/studentService.ts
```

```typescript
interface Student {
    id: number;
    name: string;
}

export class StudentService {
    private students: Student[] = [];

    addStudent(student: Student): void {
        this.students.push(student);
    }

    getStudents(): Student[] {
        return this.students;
    }

    findStudentById(id: number): Student | undefined {
        return this.students.find(student => student.id === id);
    }
}
```

Then, we will create the test file **studentService.test.ts**

```typescript
// src/services/studentService.test.ts

import { StudentService } from './studentService';

describe('StudentService', () => {
  let service: StudentService;

  beforeEach(() => {
    service = new StudentService();
  });

  it('should add a student', () => {
    const student = { id: 1, name: 'Liam' };
    service.addStudent(student);
    const students = service.getStudents();
    expect(students).toContainEqual(student);
  });

  it('should find a student by ID', () => {
    const student = { id: 2, name: 'Sophia' };
    service.addStudent(student);
```

```
    const foundStudent = service.findStudentById(2);

    expect(foundStudent).toEqual(student);

  });


  it('should return undefined for a non-existent student ID', () => {

    const foundStudent = service.findStudentById(3);

    expect(foundStudent).toBeUndefined();

  });
});
```

In the above code, we define a **StudentService** class in **studentService.ts** and write integration tests for it in **studentService.test.ts**. The tests verify that the service can add students, retrieve them, and find students by ID. The **beforeEach** function initializes the service before each test, ensuring that tests are independent and do not affect each other.

Summary

To summarize, this chapter explored the integration of TypeScript with current frameworks as well as the migration of JavaScript applications to highlight TypeScript's practical uses. The chapter began with the integration of TypeScript into Angular applications, where TypeScript's static typing and interfaces aided component and service development, resulting in better code organization and maintenance. The method involved creating an Angular project with the Angular CLI, designing TypeScript-based components, and managing services to efficiently encapsulate business logic.

The chapter then went into detail about integrating TypeScript with React, emphasizing how TypeScript improves React development by providing improved type safety and tool support. It addressed how to create a React project using Create React App and how to use TypeScript to define props, state, and hooks in functional components. This integration demonstrated TypeScript's benefits for managing complicated user interfaces and ensuring robust application behavior. The chapter also covered transitioning existing JavaScript apps to TypeScript and provided a step-by-step roadmap to ensure a smooth transition. This method included installing

TypeScript, renaming JavaScript files, adding type annotations, and addressing third-party libraries. Troubleshooting recommendations were provided to address common migration issues, such as type mismatches and missing type definitions.

Finally, the chapter taught testing TypeScript applications with the Jest framework. The use of Jest for TypeScript projects was highlighted, as well as the creation of unit and integration tests to ensure application functionality. Each function was tested independently in unit tests, and the proper interaction between components and services was verified via integration tests.

Chapter 8: Runtime Behavior and Type Checking

Chapter Overview

This final chapter will go over the runtime behavior of TypeScript applications and the different ways TypeScript improves type safety. This chapter will look at the complexities of runtime type checking, including how TypeScript's static type system interacts with JavaScript's dynamic nature. We will look at cases in which TypeScript's type checks occur during compilation and the implications for runtime behavior, which will help us comprehend the distinction between TypeScript's compile-time safety and JavaScript's runtime execution.

The chapter will cover type narrowing techniques that enable developers to refine types based on criteria, such as type guards and discriminated unions. Type narrowing allows us to use TypeScript's type inference features to construct more precise and error-free code. We will also look at the TypeScript compiler parameters, which control how TypeScript code is compiled and checked. This includes setting up the compiler to impose tougher type checks, optimize code efficiency, and produce output that meets our project needs. Understanding these options allows us to personalize the development environment to our individual requirements, improving development efficiency and code quality.

Finally, the chapter will cover how to handle asynchronous code and manage failures in TypeScript applications. Asynchronous programming is a vital component of current JavaScript development, and we will look at how TypeScript handles asynchronous processes using async/await syntax and Promises. We will also learn about error handling and exception management solutions, which will help us ensure that our applications handle unexpected events gracefully and provide useful user feedback.

Understanding Runtime Type Checking

Type checking is a fundamental aspect of programming languages that ensures variables, functions, and expressions are used consistently according to their defined types. In TypeScript, type checking primarily occurs at compile time, meaning TypeScript validates the types before the code is executed. This provides a layer of safety and predictability, allowing developers to catch potential errors early in the development process. However, TypeScript code ultimately compiles down to JavaScript, which is a dynamically typed language. This means that type checking at runtime requires additional handling since JavaScript itself does not enforce types.

What is Type Checking?

Type checking refers to the process of verifying that variables and expressions in a program conform to the expected types. In statically typed languages like TypeScript, this checking happens at compile time, where the compiler ensures that the types are consistent. This helps prevent errors such as passing a string where a number is expected or invoking a method that doesn't exist on a particular object.

In TypeScript, type annotations allow developers to explicitly specify the types of variables and function parameters. TypeScript also performs type inference, automatically determining the types based on the context. While this compile-time type checking catches many potential issues, there are cases where runtime type checking is necessary to handle dynamic data or interactions with external APIs.

Performing Type Checking at Runtime

Since TypeScript compiles to JavaScript, runtime type checking involves writing code that verifies types during execution. This is particularly useful when dealing with data from external sources, such as APIs, where the type of incoming data may be uncertain. Runtime type checking can be implemented using JavaScript's dynamic type capabilities and TypeScript's type guards.

Consider a scenario where you receive user data from an API, and you need to ensure that the data conforms to a specific type.

Define the Expected Type

```
interface User {
  id: number;
  name: string;
  email: string;
}
```

Create a Type Guard Function

Type guards are functions that determine whether a value matches a specific type.

```
function isUser(data: any): data is User {
  return (
    typeof data === 'object' &&
    typeof data.id === 'number' &&
    typeof data.name === 'string' &&
    typeof data.email === 'string'
```

```
  );
}
```

In the above code, the **isUser** function checks whether the **data** object has the expected properties and types. It returns **true** if the data matches the **User** type, enabling type-safe handling of the data.

Use the Type Guard for Runtime Checking

```
function handleApiResponse(response: any) {
  if (isUser(response)) {
    console.log(`User ID: ${response.id}`);
    console.log(`User Name: ${response.name}`);
    console.log(`User Email: ${response.email}`);
  } else {
    console.error('Invalid user data:', response);
  }
}


// Simulate an API response
const apiResponse = {
  id: 123,
  name: 'Alice',
  email: 'alice@example.com'
};
```

```
handleApiResponse(apiResponse);
```

In the above code, the **handleApiResponse** function uses the **isUser** type guard to check whether the **response** object conforms to the **User** type. If the type check passes, the function logs the user details; otherwise, it logs an error.

Troubleshooting and Managing Type Errors

Even with TypeScript's compile-time checks, runtime type errors can occur, especially when dealing with dynamic data or third-party libraries. Given below are some strategies to troubleshoot and manage type errors effectively:

Validate External Data

When working with external data sources such as APIs, validate the data before processing it. This can involve using type guards, as shown earlier, or employing libraries like io-ts or zod for more robust validation.

```
import * as t from 'io-ts';


const UserCodec = t.type({
    id: t.number,
    name: t.string,
    email: t.string
});


type User = t.TypeOf<typeof UserCodec>;


function validateUser(data: unknown): User | null {
    const result = UserCodec.decode(data);
```

```
  if (result._tag === 'Right') {
    return result.right;
  } else {
    console.error('Validation error:', result.left);
    return null;
  }
}

const apiResponse = {
  id: 123,
  name: 'Alice',
  email: 'alice@example.com'
};

const user = validateUser(apiResponse);
if (user) {
  console.log('Validated User:', user);
}
```

In the above code, the **io-ts** library is used to define a codec for the **User** type and validate the **apiResponse**. If the validation is successful, the user object is returned; otherwise, an error is logged.

Use Fallbacks for Undefined or Null Values

JavaScript and TypeScript allow **undefined** and **null** values, which can lead to runtime errors if not handled properly. Use optional chaining and nullish coalescing to manage these values gracefully.

```
function getUserEmail(user: User | null): string {
  return user?.email ?? 'Email not available';
}
```

```
const user = { id: 1, name: 'Bob', email: 'bob@example.com' };
console.log(getUserEmail(user)); // Output: bob@example.com
```

```
const unknownUser = null;
console.log(getUserEmail(unknownUser)); // Output: Email not available
```

In the above code, optional chaining (**user?.email**) safely accesses the email property, and nullish coalescing (**??**) provides a default value if the email is undefined or null.

Implement Error Handling Mechanisms

Incorporate error handling mechanisms such as try-catch blocks to capture and manage runtime errors.

```
function parseJson(jsonString: string): any {
  try {
    return JSON.parse(jsonString);
  } catch (error) {
```

```
    console.error('Failed to parse JSON:', error);
    return null;
  }
}


const jsonString = '{"id": 1, "name": "Charlie"}';
const parsedData = parseJson(jsonString);
if (parsedData) {
  console.log('Parsed Data:', parsedData);
}
```

In the above code, the **parseJson** function attempts to parse a JSON string and catches any parsing errors using a try-catch block. This prevents the application from crashing due to invalid JSON input.

Leverage TypeScript Compiler Options

Configure the TypeScript compiler to enforce stricter type checks and catch potential errors during development.

```
{
  "compilerOptions": {
    "strict": true,
    "noImplicitAny": true,
    "strictNullChecks": true,
    "strictPropertyInitialization": true
  }
}
```

In the above code, enabling strict mode and specific compiler options in **tsconfig.json** enhances type safety by disallowing implicit **any** types and requiring explicit handling of null and undefined values.

Document and Communicate Type Expectations

Document the expected types of functions, interfaces, and data structures using comments and documentation tools. This improves communication among developers and ensures that everyone understands the intended use of the code.

```
/**
 * Represents a user in the system.
 */
interface User {
    id: number; // Unique identifier for the user
    name: string; // Name of the user
    email: string; // Email address of the user
}


/**
 * Retrieves a user by ID.
 * @param id - The ID of the user to retrieve.
 * @returns The user with the specified ID, or undefined if not found.
 */
function getUserById(id: number): User | undefined {
```

```
  // Implementation here
}
```

In the above code, documentation comments are added to the **User** interface and **getUserById** function, providing clear information about the types and parameters.

Type Narrowing Techniques

Type narrowing is a key feature that allows developers to refine types based on runtime information and control flow analysis. By narrowing types, developers can ensure that code operates on the expected data type, reducing the likelihood of runtime errors. TypeScript's ability to infer and narrow types makes it a powerful tool for managing complex data structures and ensuring that code is type-safe and robust.

What is Type Narrowing?

Type narrowing refers to the process of refining a broader or more general type to a more specific one based on certain conditions or operations in your code. This allows developers to apply specific logic to certain types, reducing the risk of runtime errors caused by unexpected data types.

For example, consider a function that can accept both strings and numbers. Type narrowing allows you to apply different logic based on whether the input is a string or a number.

```
function processInput(input: string | number) {
  if (typeof input === 'string') {
    console.log(`Input is a string of length ${input.length}`);
  } else {
    console.log(`Input is a number: ${input.toFixed(2)}`);
  }
}
```

```
processInput('Hello'); // Output: Input is a string of
length 5

processInput(3.14159); // Output: Input is a number: 3.14
```

In the above code, the type of **input** is narrowed to **string** or **number** based on the **typeof** check. This allows TypeScript to provide accurate type-specific functionality, such as accessing the **length** property for strings and calling **toFixed** for numbers.

Type Narrowing Techniques

TypeScript offers several techniques for type narrowing, including type guards, control flow analysis, and discriminated unions. These techniques help refine types in a variety of situations, allowing developers to write precise and reliable code.

Type Guards

Type guards are expressions used to narrow down the type of a variable within a conditional block. They are often used with **typeof** and **instanceof** operators, as well as user-defined type guard functions.

- Using **typeof** for Primitives

The **typeof** operator is commonly used to narrow types of primitive values like **string**, **number**, and **boolean**.

```
function printLength(value: string | number) {
  if (typeof value === 'string') {
    console.log(`String length: ${value.length}`);
  } else {
    console.log(`Number: ${value}`);
  }
}
```

In the above code, **typeof value** is used to check if **value** is a **string** or **number**, allowing the code to handle each case appropriately.

- Using **instanceof** for Objects

The **instanceof** operator is used to narrow types of objects based on their constructor.

```
class Dog {

  bark() {

    console.log('Woof!');

  }

}


class Cat {

  meow() {

    console.log('Meow!');

  }

}


function makeSound(animal: Dog | Cat) {

  if (animal instanceof Dog) {

    animal.bark();

  } else {

    animal.meow();

  }

}
```

```
makeSound(new Dog()); // Output: Woof!

makeSound(new Cat()); // Output: Meow!
```

In the above code, **instanceof** is used to determine if **animal** is an instance of **Dog** or **Cat**, allowing the correct method to be called.

- User-Defined Type Guards

User-defined type guards are functions that return a boolean value indicating whether a value matches a specific type. They are useful for more complex type checks.

```
interface Car {
  drive(): void;
}


interface Boat {
  sail(): void;
}


function isCar(vehicle: Car | Boat): vehicle is Car {
  return (vehicle as Car).drive !== undefined;
}


function operateVehicle(vehicle: Car | Boat) {
  if (isCar(vehicle)) {
    vehicle.drive();
  } else {
```

```
    vehicle.sail();
  }
}


const car: Car = { drive: () => console.log('Driving') };
const boat: Boat = { sail: () => console.log('Sailing') };


operateVehicle(car);  // Output: Driving

operateVehicle(boat); // Output: Sailing
```

In the above code, the **isCar** function serves as a user-defined type guard, determining if **vehicle** is a **Car**. The function checks if the **drive** method is defined, allowing TypeScript to narrow the type accordingly.

Control Flow Analysis

TypeScript uses control flow analysis to refine types based on the flow of the code. This analysis considers the path that the code takes, allowing TypeScript to narrow types more precisely.

- Narrowing with **if** Statements

TypeScript narrows types within **if** statements by analyzing the conditions.

```
function checkValue(value: number | null) {
  if (value !== null) {
    console.log(`Value is a number: ${value.toFixed(2)}`);
  } else {
    console.log('Value is null');
```

```
    }
}
```

```
checkValue(42); // Output: Value is a number: 42.00
checkValue(null); // Output: Value is null
```

In the above code, TypeScript recognizes that **value** is not **null** within the **if** block, allowing **toFixed** to be safely called.

- Narrowing with **switch** Statements

TypeScript can also narrow types within **switch** statements.

```
type Shape = 'circle' | 'square';

function calculateArea(shape: Shape, size: number) {
  switch (shape) {
    case 'circle':
      return Math.PI * size * size;
    case 'square':
      return size * size;
  }
}

console.log(calculateArea('circle', 3)); // Output: 28.274333882308138
```

```
console.log(calculateArea('square', 3)); // Output: 9
```

In the above code, the **shape** type is narrowed within each **case** block, allowing TypeScript to infer the correct type for calculations.

- Narrowing with Loops

TypeScript can narrow types within loops, considering the loop's exit conditions.

```
function findFirstPositive(numbers: (number | null)[]):
number | undefined {

  for (const num of numbers) {

    if (num !== null && num > 0) {

      return num;

    }

  }

  return undefined;

}


const numbers = [null, -1, 0, 5, null];

console.log(findFirstPositive(numbers)); // Output: 5
```

In the above code, TypeScript narrows **num** to **number** within the loop, allowing the comparison with **0**.

Discriminated Unions

Discriminated unions are a powerful pattern that use a common property to differentiate between union members. They enable more precise type narrowing.

```
interface Circle {

  kind: 'circle';
```

```
  radius: number;
}

interface Square {
  kind: 'square';
  sideLength: number;
}

type Shape = Circle | Square;

function getArea(shape: Shape) {
  switch (shape.kind) {
    case 'circle':
      return Math.PI * shape.radius * shape.radius;
    case 'square':
      return shape.sideLength * shape.sideLength;
  }
}

const circle: Circle = { kind: 'circle', radius: 2 };
const square: Square = { kind: 'square', sideLength: 2 };
```

```
console.log(getArea(circle)); // Output:
12.566370614359172

console.log(getArea(square)); // Output: 4
```

In the above code, the **kind** property serves as a discriminant, allowing TypeScript to narrow the type of **shape** within the **switch** statement. Type narrowing is a crucial technique that enhances type safety and reduces runtime errors. By leveraging type guards, control flow analysis, and discriminated unions, developers can write more precise and reliable code, ensuring that operations are performed on the correct data types.

Handling Asynchronous Code

Asynchronous programming is a critical aspect of modern JavaScript and TypeScript development. It allows applications to perform long-running tasks, such as fetching data from a server, without blocking the main execution thread. This ensures that applications remain responsive and efficient, even when dealing with complex operations. In this section, we will explore the fundamentals of asynchronous programming using Promises and the **async/await** syntax. We will also cover troubleshooting techniques for handling errors in asynchronous code.

Introduction to Promises

Promises are a key feature of JavaScript that represent the eventual completion or failure of an asynchronous operation. They provide a clean and readable way to handle asynchronous tasks, enabling developers to write more manageable code.

Creating a Promise

A Promise can be created using the **Promise** constructor, which takes a function as an argument. This function receives two parameters: **resolve** and **reject**. These parameters are functions used to mark the Promise as fulfilled or rejected, respectively.

```
const myPromise = new Promise<string>((resolve, reject) => {
  const success = true;
```

```
    if (success) {

      resolve('Operation succeeded');

    } else {

      reject('Operation failed');

    }

  });


myPromise

  .then(result => console.log(result))

  .catch(error => console.error(error));
```

In the above code, the Promise is resolved with a success message if the operation succeeds and rejected with an error message if it fails. The **then** method handles the resolved value, while the **catch** method handles the rejected value.

Chaining Promises

Promises can be chained together to perform sequential asynchronous operations. Each **then** call returns a new Promise, allowing multiple operations to be linked.

```
function fetchData(): Promise<string> {

  return new Promise((resolve) => {

    setTimeout(() => resolve('Data fetched'), 1000);

  });

}



function processData(data: string): Promise<string> {
```

```
  return new Promise((resolve) => {
    setTimeout(() => resolve(`${data} processed`), 1000);
  });
}


fetchData()
  .then(result => processData(result))
  .then(finalResult => console.log(finalResult))
  .catch(error => console.error(error));
```

In the above code, **fetchData** returns a Promise that resolves with a data string after 1 second. The resolved value is then passed to **processData**, which returns another Promise that processes the data. The final result is logged to the console.

Async/Await Syntax

The **async/await** syntax provides a more concise and readable way to work with Promises. It allows developers to write asynchronous code that looks synchronous, making it easier to understand and maintain.

Using Async/Await

To use **async/await**, declare a function as **async** and use the **await** keyword to pause execution until a Promise is resolved or rejected.

```
async function performAsyncOperations() {
  try {
    const data = await fetchData();
    const processedData = await processData(data);
    console.log(processedData);
```

```
  } catch (error) {
    console.error(error);
  }
}

performAsyncOperations();
```

In the above code, the **performAsyncOperations** function is marked as **async**, allowing the use of **await** to pause execution until each Promise is resolved. The **try/catch** block handles any errors that occur during the asynchronous operations.

Working with Multiple Promises

async/await can be used with multiple Promises, enabling parallel execution and improved performance.

```
async function fetchMultipleData() {
  try {
    const [data1, data2] = await Promise.all([fetchData(), processData('Sample')]);
    console.log('Data 1:', data1);
    console.log('Data 2:', data2);
  } catch (error) {
    console.error(error);
  }
}
```

```
fetchMultipleData();
```

In the above code, **Promise.all** is used to execute **fetchData** and **processData** in parallel. The results are returned as an array, allowing both operations to be completed before processing the results.

Troubleshooting Errors in Asynchronous Code

Asynchronous code can introduce new challenges when it comes to error handling and debugging. Understanding how to effectively manage errors is crucial for building robust and reliable applications.

Handling Promise Rejections

Unhandled Promise rejections can lead to unexpected behavior and application crashes. Use the **catch** method or a **try/catch** block to handle rejections.

```
myPromise
    .then(result => console.log(result))
    .catch(error => console.error('Promise rejected:', error));
```

In the above code, the **catch** method ensures that any rejected Promises are handled gracefully.

Using Try/Catch with Async/Await

When using **async/await**, wrap asynchronous operations in a **try/catch** block to manage errors.

```
async function fetchDataWithError() {
  throw new Error('Failed to fetch data');
}


async function handleData() {
  try {
```

```
    const data = await fetchDataWithError();

    console.log(data);

  } catch (error) {

    console.error('Error fetching data:', error);

  }

}


handleData();
```

In the above code, an error is thrown in the **fetchDataWithError** function. The **try/catch** block in **handleData** catches the error and logs it to the console.

Debugging Asynchronous Code

Debugging asynchronous code can be challenging due to the non-linear execution flow. Use logging, breakpoints, and specialized tools to diagnose issues.

```
async function debugAsyncOperations() {

    console.log('Starting operations');

    const data = await fetchData();

    console.log('Data fetched:', data);

    const processedData = await processData(data);

    console.log('Data processed:', processedData);

}


debugAsyncOperations();
```

In the above code, console logging is used to trace the flow of asynchronous operations, helping to identify where issues may occur.

Managing Timeouts and Race Conditions

Asynchronous operations may encounter timeouts or race conditions, leading to inconsistent results. Implement timeouts and ensure that operations complete in the desired order.

```
function fetchDataWithTimeout(): Promise<string> {
  return new Promise((resolve, reject) => {
    setTimeout(() => resolve('Data fetched with delay'), 2000);
    setTimeout(() => reject('Timeout error'), 1000);
  });
}


async function fetchDataSafely() {
  try {
    const data = await fetchDataWithTimeout();
    console.log(data);
  } catch (error) {
    console.error('Error:', error);
  }
}


fetchDataSafely();
```

In the above code, a Promise with a longer delay is rejected due to a timeout, demonstrating the importance of managing time-sensitive operations.

Handling Network Errors

Network errors can occur when making API calls or interacting with external services. Implement retries or fallback mechanisms to handle these scenarios.

```
async function fetchDataWithRetry(attempts: number = 3): Promise<string> {
  for (let i = 0; i < attempts; i++) {
    try {
      const data = await fetchData();
      return data;
    } catch (error) {
      console.warn(`Attempt ${i + 1} failed:`, error);
      if (i === attempts - 1) throw new Error('All attempts failed');
    }
  }
}

fetchDataWithRetry()
  .then(data => console.log('Data fetched:', data))
  .catch(error => console.error('Final error:', error));
```

In the above code, the **fetchDataWithRetry** function attempts to fetch data multiple times before ultimately failing, providing resilience against transient network issues.

Developers may create dependable, responsive, and strong apps that handle asynchronous operations gracefully if they understand these ideas and use efficient error-handling mechanisms.

Exception Management

Exception management is a critical aspect of software development that involves handling errors and unexpected situations gracefully. In TypeScript, exception management ensures that applications continue to function even when unexpected issues arise, providing a better user experience and more robust applications. This section will explore how to use **try/catch** blocks for exception management and how to create custom error classes to handle specific error scenarios more effectively.

Introduction to Try/Catch Blocks

The **try/catch** block is a fundamental construct in JavaScript and TypeScript for managing exceptions. It allows developers to execute a block of code and catch any errors that occur within that block. By handling exceptions, you can prevent your application from crashing and provide meaningful error messages or recovery mechanisms.

Using Try/Catch Blocks

A **try/catch** block consists of two main parts: the **try** block, which contains the code that might throw an error, and the **catch** block, which handles the error if it occurs.

```
try {
  // Code that might throw an error
} catch (error) {
  // Handle the error
}
```

Consider a scenario where you need to parse JSON data, which might be malformed and cause an error.

```
function parseJson(jsonString: string): any {
  try {
    const data = JSON.parse(jsonString);
```

```
    console.log('Parsed data:', data);

    return data;

  } catch (error) {

    console.error('Failed to parse JSON:', error);

    return null;

  }

}

const validJson = '{"id": 1, "name": "Alice"}';
const invalidJson = '{"id": 1, "name": "Alice"';


parseJson(validJson); // Output: Parsed data: { id: 1, name: 'Alice' }

parseJson(invalidJson); // Output: Failed to parse JSON: [SyntaxError: Unexpected end of JSON input]
```

In the above code, the **parseJson** function uses a **try/catch** block to handle potential errors when parsing a JSON string. If an error occurs, it is caught in the **catch** block, allowing the function to log the error and return **null** instead of crashing the application.

Handling Specific Errors

You can customize the **catch** block to handle specific error types or conditions. This allows you to provide more targeted error messages or recovery mechanisms.

```
function divideNumbers(a: number, b: number): number {
  try {
    if (b === 0) {
```

```
      throw new Error('Division by zero');
    }
    return a / b;
  } catch (error) {
    console.error('Error:', error.message);
    return NaN;
  }
}

console.log(divideNumbers(10, 2)); // Output: 5

console.log(divideNumbers(10, 0)); // Output: Error: Division by zero
```

In the above code, the **divideNumbers** function throws an error if a division by zero is attempted. The **catch** block handles this specific error and logs a meaningful message.

Creating Custom Error Classes

While built-in error types like **Error**, **TypeError**, and **RangeError** cover many common scenarios, creating custom error classes allows you to define application-specific errors. Custom error classes help you encapsulate additional information and provide more detailed error handling.

Defining Custom Error Class

To create a custom error class, extend the built-in **Error** class and add any additional properties or methods needed for your specific error scenario.

```
class ValidationError extends Error {
  constructor(message: string, public invalidField: string) {
```

```
    super(message);
    this.name = 'ValidationError';
  }
}
```

In the above code, the **ValidationError** class extends the **Error** class and includes an additional property, **invalidField**, to specify which field caused the validation error.

Using Custom Error Classes

Custom error classes can be used to throw and catch specific errors in your application.

```
function validateUser(user: { name: string; email: string }) {
  if (!user.name) {
    throw new ValidationError('Name is required', 'name');
  }
  if (!user.email) {
    throw new ValidationError('Email is required', 'email');
  }
  console.log('User is valid:', user);
}

try {
  validateUser({ name: '', email: 'alice@example.com' });
```

```
  } catch (error) {
    if (error instanceof ValidationError) {
      console.error(`Validation error on field ${error.invalidField}: ${error.message}`);
    } else {
      console.error('Unexpected error:', error);
    }
  }
}
```

In the above code, the **validateUser** function throws a **ValidationError** if the user's name or email is missing. The **try/catch** block handles this specific error type, providing detailed information about the validation error.

Handling Multiple Error Types

When dealing with multiple error types, use conditional logic in the **catch** block to handle each type appropriately.

```
class NetworkError extends Error {
  constructor(message: string, public url: string) {
    super(message);
    this.name = 'NetworkError';
  }
}


async function fetchData(url: string) {
  try {
```

```
    // Simulate a network error
    throw new NetworkError('Failed to fetch data', url);
  } catch (error) {
    if (error instanceof NetworkError) {
      console.error(`Network error when fetching ${error.url}: ${error.message}`);
    } else {
      console.error('Unexpected error:', error);
    }
  }
}

fetchData('https://api.example.com/data');
```

In the above code, the **fetchData** function throws a **NetworkError** when a network-related issue occurs. The **catch** block differentiates between **NetworkError** and other error types, providing specific error handling for each case.

Propagating Errors

In some cases, it may be appropriate to propagate an error to a higher-level function instead of handling it immediately. This allows centralized error handling or logging.

```
function fetchDataWithError() {
  throw new Error('Network error');
}
```

```
function getData() {
  try {
    fetchDataWithError();
  } catch (error) {
    console.error('Error fetching data:', error);
    throw error; // Propagate the error to the caller
  }
}

try {
  getData();
} catch (error) {
  console.error('Error in application:', error);
}
```

In the above code, the **getData** function catches the error from **fetchDataWithError** and logs it, but then rethrows the error to be handled by a higher-level function. This approach allows for more flexible error management strategies.

Summary

In conclusion, this chapter covered the essentials of TypeScript's runtime behavior and type checking, which improved our knowledge of how to create efficient and reliable applications. The first part of the chapter focused on runtime type checking, which drew attention to the fact that runtime types are different from compile-time types. It demonstrated how TypeScript uses type guards, such as **typeof**, **instanceof**, and custom type guard functions, to narrow down types and ensure type safety. This process enabled developers to handle dynamic data and interactions with external APIs more effectively.

The chapter further took us to type narrowing techniques, focusing on control flow analysis. Through the use of conditional statements, loops, and discriminated unions, TypeScript's control flow analysis allowed types to be refined based on code paths. This provided a robust mechanism for handling various data structures and improving code reliability by ensuring operations were performed on the expected types. The chapter then addressed asynchronous programming with Promises and the `async/await` syntax, crucial for managing long-running tasks without blocking execution. It covered creating and chaining Promises, using `async/await` for a more readable asynchronous code structure, and handling multiple asynchronous operations. Additionally, it taught troubleshooting asynchronous code, including managing Promise rejections, handling network errors, and avoiding race conditions.

Finally, exception management was covered, focusing on using `try/catch` blocks for error handling and creating custom error classes to encapsulate specific error scenarios. This allowed for targeted error handling and better application stability. This chapter taught readers how to handle exceptions with grace, which is crucial for making sure applications can handle unexpected problems while still being user-friendly. Overarchingly, this chapter elucidated runtime behavior and type safety in great detail, highlighting the significance of error handling and type management in TypeScript applications.

Index

A

Advanced Object Types 112
Angular 2, 216, 217, 219, 220, 222, 223, 224, 246, 252
Angular Components 217, 222
Angular Directives 223
Angular Pipes 224
Angular Services 219
APIs 63, 246, 256, 258, 286
Array Type 15
Arrow Functions 53, 67, 68, 69
Async/Await 273, 275

B

Basic Types 25
Boolean Type 26

C

Classes 86, 124, 125, 141, 153, 154
Compilation 8, 19, 20, 242
Control Flow Analysis 267
Custom Error Classes 281, 282

D

Debugging 276
Default Export 190, 196
Default Parameters 56, 58
Discriminated Unions 269

E

Enum Type 36
Error Handling 260
Exception Management 279

F

Function Types 16, 51

I

Index Signatures 112, 113, 114
Inheritance 125, 138, 145
Integration 246, 249

I

Integration Test 249
Interfaces 124, 125, 153, 154, 169, 171, 173, 185
Intersection Types 78, 81, 82, 173

J

Jest 246, 247, 248, 253

L

Literal Types 92, 93

M

Migration 4, 238, 242, 243
Modules 122, 187, 188, 192, 193, 194, 195, 198

N

Named Export 189, 195, 201
Namespaces 187, 188, 205, 207, 208, 209, 212
Network Errors 278
Node.js 2, 4, 5, 8, 24, 216, 217, 247
Nullable Types 100, 101

O

Optional Parameters 56
Optional Properties 100, 103, 105, 158

P

Private Modifier 132
Promises 255, 271, 272, 273, 274, 275, 286
Protected Modifier 131, 134
Public Modifier 131

R

Race Conditions 277
React 173, 176, 185, 216, 225, 226, 227, 228, 229, 230, 231, 232, 233, 234, 236, 237, 246, 252
React Components 226
React Context 233, 237
React Hooks 230
Recursive Types 115, 116
Rest Parameters 60, 62
Runtime Behavior 254

Runtime Errors 243

T

Try/Catch.. 275, 279
tsconfig.json...... 5, 6, 8, 20, 21, 22, 23, 24, 27, 188, 214, 238, 262
Tuple Type 15, 32
Type Aliases.. 92, 94, 95, 97
Type Annotations................................... 11, 14, 15, 18, 239
Type Assertions 85, 89, 91
Type Checking 20, 239, 254, 255, 256
Type Guard......................... 45, 85, 86, 256, 257, 264, 266
Type Inference 16, 17, 19, 242
Type Narrowing..263, 264
TypeScript Compiler 5, 20, 261
TypeScript Compiler Options..261

TypeScript Environment 4

U

Union Types..77, 78, 79
Unit Test 248

V

Void Type 40

W

Web Development 116

Epilogue

Just before we wrap up "Learning TypeScript 5," I'd like to take a moment to reflect on everything we've covered so far. Moving from JavaScript to TypeScript has been a rewarding experience for me, and I hope it is for you as well. My goal has always been to provide you with the knowledge and skills necessary to fully utilize TypeScript's capabilities in your projects. If you're writing cleaner, more reliable code and feeling more confident about your development work, this book has served its purpose. Throughout this book, we've looked at the fundamental features and benefits of TypeScript, from setting up your development environment to mastering advanced concepts like type narrowing and asynchronous programming. Along the way, we faced practical challenges and used TypeScript in real-world scenarios. Using a hands-on approach, you've witnessed firsthand how TypeScript improves code quality, reduces errors, and simplifies complex development tasks.

I'd like to share a personal story that demonstrates why I am so passionate about TypeScript. Recently, I collaborated with a small startup team on a fast-paced project. We were tasked with delivering a feature-rich application within a tight timeframe. Initially, the team was hesitant to introduce TypeScript, fearing it would slow us down. However, we decided to try it, and the results were fantastic. TypeScript not only helped us detect errors earlier, but it also improved team collaboration. Everyone on the team, regardless of project experience, could easily understand the code thanks to TypeScript's clear type definitions and interfaces. During a critical phase, we discovered an unexpected bug that could delay our release. We were able to quickly identify and resolve the issue using TypeScript, saving us valuable time. The confidence that TypeScript instilled in our development process was incredible. We were able to deliver the application on time, and our clients were extremely pleased with the outcome. This experience reinforced my belief that TypeScript is more than a tool; it is a game changer for developers.

As you progress in software development, I encourage you to continue exploring and experimenting with TypeScript. The language is constantly evolving, and staying current on the latest features and best practices will keep you at the cutting edge of modern web development. Because of TypeScript's expanding ecosystem, there are always new tools and libraries to discover, improving your ability to create robust and scalable applications. I hope this book has not only provided you with technical knowledge, but also inspired you to take on new challenges and opportunities. Whether you're creating complex enterprise applications or simple personal projects, TypeScript provides a powerful framework to help you succeed. Thank you for choosing to learn TypeScript alongside me. I'm looking forward to seeing how you use what you've learned to develop innovative and impactful solutions. As you progress, keep in mind that the skills you've learned are a solid foundation for success in the ever-changing world of technology.

Continue coding, exploring, and, most importantly, enjoying the process.

Thank You

Made in the USA
Monee, IL
03 May 2026

49438693R00168